THE
LITTLE BOOK OF
PICKLEBALL

LAURA FRANCIS

First published in Great Britain in 2025 by
Cassell, an imprint of
Octopus Publishing Group Ltd,
Carmelite House,
50 Victoria Embankment,
London EC4Y 0DZ
www.octopusbooks.co.uk

An Hachette UK Company
www.hachette.co.uk

ISBN 978-1-788-40521-8
A CIP catalogue record for this book is available from the British Library.
Printed and bound in the China
10 9 8 7 6 5 4 3 2 1

Produced for Octopus by Imago Create

Publisher: Trevor Davies
Assistant Editor: Stephanie Selcuk-Frank
Designer: Gary Hyde
Editor: Jon Richards
Consultant: Bob Hutchinson
Proofreader: Katie Dicker
Senior Production Manager: Peter Hunt
Artists: Niall Harding and Gemma Hastilow (Beehive Illustration)

This FSC® label means that materials used for
the product have been responsibly sourced.

MIX
Paper | Supporting
responsible forestry
FSC® C016973
FSC
www.fsc.org

THE
LITTLE BOOK OF
PICKLEBALL

The Essential Pickler's Guide to the Fastest-Growing Sport in the World

LAURA FRANCIS

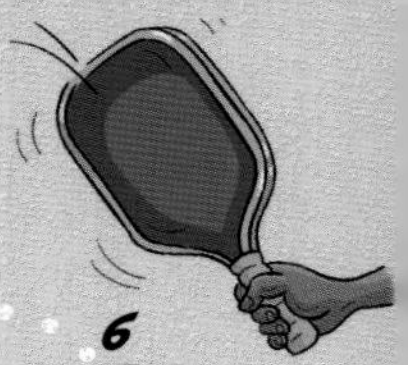

CONTENTS

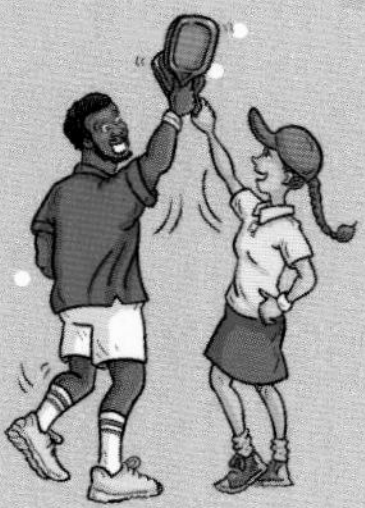

**'I'VE HEARD
PEOPLE SAY IT'S LIKE
PING PONG
ON STEROIDS.'**

– Pro pickler Tyson McGuffin

CHAPTER ONE

THE BIRTH OF PICKLEBALL

Perhaps you bought this book for yourself. Perhaps a pickling pal lent it to you, trying to bring you into the fold. Maybe a cherished friend or relative gave it to you, noticing your newfound obsession with the sport. Whether you're a casual dinker or have a full-blown dinking problem, this book is for you. So, sit back and enjoy.

Let's start at the beginning, with the birth of the most addictive sport on Earth...

THE ORIGIN OF PICKLEBALL

The story of pickleball begins mere decades ago, and yet it has already become the stuff of legend. Were it not for some missing badminton equipment, then perhaps this wondrous game would never have been invented.

The year was 1965. The place was Bainbridge Island, Washington State. Congressman Joel Pritchard and his friend Bill Bell had spent a pleasant summer morning playing golf. When they returned home, they found their families at a loose end. Inspired to play badminton on the property's courts, their attempts were scuppered when they couldn't find enough rackets.

However, the creative pair were not going to let that stand in their way. Instead, they gathered some ping pong paddles and a plastic wiffle ball and set about making up their own game. It was a bit like tennis, mixed with badminton, mixed with ping pong.
It turned out to be pretty good family fun. Perhaps, they mused, they're on to something...

Not wanting to let a good idea go to waste, the two sportsmen continued to refine the rules of their new game and introduced it to their friend Barney McCallum, who got to work designing the first official pickleball paddles.

In the years that followed, the game that started off as an idle summer pursuit grew into an official sport, with the very first tournament taking place in 1976. By 1990, it was being played in all 50 U.S. states, and its meteoric rise in popularity during the 21st century has seen people dinking and lobbing around the world.

So, ladies and gentlemen, please raise your paddles and celebrate the sporting geniuses Pritchard, McCallum and Bell, creators of the USA's fastest growing sport!

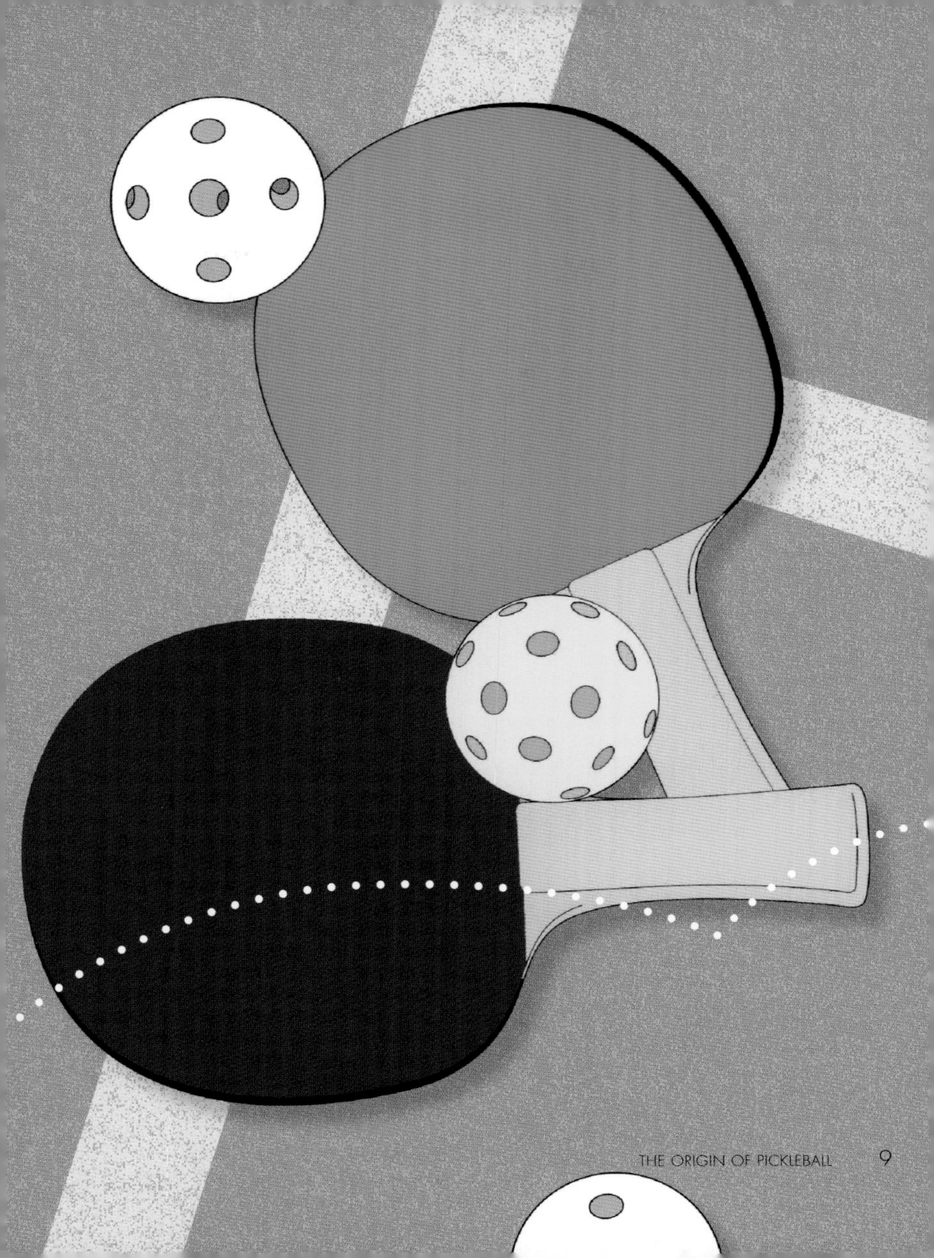

WHAT'S IN A NAME?

You've got to admit – love it or hate it – 'pickleball' is a memorable name. There's nothing else quite like it. The 'ball' bit makes sense, but what's with the pickle? Did the game's inventors run out of balls as well as badminton rackets and decide that a dill pickle would do the job?

As with all good creation stories, it can be tricky to unpick fact from fiction. Many have claimed that Joel Pritchard named his new sport 'pickleball' after the family dog, Pickles. However, the Pritchards soon set the record straight: the pooch was named after the game.

'IT WAS NOT NAMED AFTER THE DOG BECAUSE WE DIDN'T GET THE DOG UNTIL YEARS AFTER THE GAME STARTED. THE DOG WAS NAMED AFTER THE GAME. NOT THE OTHER WAY AROUND.'
– Pritchard's daughter, Peggy

LET'S CALL IT...

TENNY PONG? NO.

So, why pickleball? Were the family gluttons for gherkins? Did they relish relish? Nope! It was Joel's wife, Joan, who christened the mash-up sport, calling it pickleball after a little-known rowing term.

'I SAID IT REMINDED ME OF THE PICKLE BOAT IN CREW WHERE OARSMEN WERE CHOSEN FROM THE LEFTOVERS OF OTHER BOATS.'

– Joan Pritchard

TENMINTON PING PADDLE? NO!

BADMY-PING PADDLE-PONG? HELL NO!

THE RISE AND RISE OF PICKLEBALL

Since that idle morning in 1965, pickleball has been drawing in new disciples. Slowly at first, as friends and neighbours were converted to the joys of the game with a silly name. Then its popularity spread further afield, travelling south with the snowbirds, those older people who found pickleball provided a gentler pace than tennis, while getting them out on a court and having fun with their friends.

As the 20th century drew to a close, pickleball had amassed a solid following, but it had few dedicated courts. If you'd picked out a person at random and asked them 'What's pickleball?' they'd likely reply that it must be some sort of savoury snack. But all that was about to change.

The thing about picklers is, they need to tell everyone how great pickleball is. They just can't help themselves. Word spread. More courts were built. Younger people tried it out. They liked it. As pro pickler Kyle Yates says, 'Who doesn't love playing this game?... It's a sport for everybody.'

1965
PICKLEBALL IS INVENTED IN WASHINGTON STATE BY PRITCHARD, BELL AND MCCALLUM.

1972
THE FOUNDERS SET UP PICKLE-BALL INC. TO PROTECT THE FLEDGLING SPORT.

1967
THE FIRST PERMANENT PICKLEBALL COURT IS BUILT IN THE BACKYARD OF PRITCHARD'S NEIGHBOUR, BOB O'BRIEN.

1976
THE FIRST PICKLEBALL TOURNAMENT TAKES PLACE IN WASHINGTON STATE.

1984
THE FIRST EDITION OF THE PICKLEBALL RULE BOOK IS PUBLISHED.

So here we are. Pickleball's seventh decade. Suddenly it seems like everyone is playing pickleball, or they're about to. With 4.8 million US players in 2022 and 8.9 million in 2023, it's officially America's fastest growing sport. And where America goes, the rest of the world often follows.

2000
THE FIRST THOUSAND TRAILS TOURNAMENT IS HELD IN CALIFORNIA.

1990
PICKLEBALL IS NOW PLAYED IN ALL 50 U.S. STATES.

2001
PICKLEBALL IS DEMONSTRATED AT THE ARIZONA SENIOR OLYMPICS.

'ON THE SAME COURT, YOU CAN HAVE A MILLIONAIRE WITH SOMEONE LIVING PAYCHECK TO PAYCHECK. NO ONE'S INTERESTED IN WHAT YOU DO FOR A LIVING, ONLY IN HOW LONG YOU'VE BEEN PLAYING.'

— Simone Jardim, pro pickleball player

CHAPTER TWO

WHY PICKLEBALL?

The fun, the camaraderie, the endorphin-releasing exercise. Let's face it, with so much going for this sport, the question should be 'Why not pickleball?' From the uber-competitive athlete to the player who just wants an excuse to socialise, there are as many types of pickleball player as there are reasons to pick up a paddle.

THE PROS AND CONS OF PICKLEBALL

There's a reason pickleball is the fastest-growing sport in the United States. Actually, there are many reasons. But in case you're trying to weigh up whether or not pickleball is worthy of your unswaying love and devotion, here is a helpful pros and cons list to help you decide.

PROS

- Any age can play – young, old and anywhere in between.

- You can play whether you are athletic or not. You don't need to be 'beach body ready' to play pickleball, you just need to be ready to have fun.

- It's easy to pick up. You'll learn the rules after just a few short games.

- It has plenty of fun slang terms and doesn't take itself seriously.

- Men and women can play together.

- You can play singles or doubles.

- You don't need expensive equipment.

- It's sociable. You're never too far away from your pickle partner.

- The low net and non-volley zone mean that height is not a major advantage.

- The small court size means you don't have to run around as much as when playing tennis.

> **'THE CAMARADERIE EXTENDS BEYOND THE COURT, FOSTERING CONNECTIONS AND FRIENDSHIPS THAT OFTEN CONTINUE OFF THE PLAYING SURFACE.'**
>
> – Pickleball record-breaker Joshua Biggers

CONS

- It's addictive. Before you know it, you'll want to pickle every day. You'll think of nothing else. You'll be lobbing and dinking in your dreams.

- Your loved ones will worry you've joined a cult.

- You'll start bunking off work to play pickleball so much that you're fired from your job.

- You'll spend your life savings on top-of-the-range equipment. 'Just one more paddle,' you'll say, as they strap you into a straightjacket. 'I really think this paddle will help me get a 4.0 rating!'

IT'S BETTER THAN A DATING APP!

In the old days, there was courting, now there's on-the-courting. If you're tired of swiping right, then put down that phone and pick up a paddle. Just picture it: your eyes meet across the net. They wow you with their cross-court dink, your footwork Ernes their admiration. The pickleball court could be the setting for your next meet.

SINGLE AND READY TO MINGLE

Pickleball enthusiasts have set up 'Single Mingle' events for picklers who are looking for love and friendship. Hundreds of players attend the events, hoping to impress with their soft serves and skilful dinks. Singles wear green wristbands, while the handful who are already taken wear red.

> YOU CAN TELL A LOT ABOUT A PERSON'S CHARACTER ON THE PICKLEBALL COURT. SHOW OFF YOUR BEST SIDE AND LOOK OUT FOR PICKLEBALL PLAYERS WHO WOW YOU WITH THEIR ATTITUDE.

WANT TO ATTRACT YOUR PERFECT PARTNER ON THE COURT?

- **DON'T** serve a Nasty Nelson. This isn't the playground and you're too big to be pulling pigtails.

- **NO POACHING.** Stop showing off and give them some space.

- **YOU TRIED A TWEENER** and fell on your butt? Laugh it off. You don't need a sore ego as well as a bruised backside.

- **DON'T TRY** to win at all costs. Good sportsmanship is your best way to impress.

- **SUGGEST** a post-match get-together, either one-on-one or as a group. You've already got pickleball in common. What else?

BACKHANDED COMPLIMENTS = BAD
COMPLIMENTING THEIR BACKHAND = GOOD

PICKLEBALL PICK-UP LINES

'YOU CAN STEP INTO MY KITCHEN ANYTIME.'

'WANNA GO FOR A DINK?'

'YOU MAKE ME FEEL LIKE I'VE WON A GOLDEN PICKLE.'

VENN PICKLEGRAMS

Pickleball is the sport that doesn't take itself too seriously. So what better way of celebrating it than with some not-so-serious Venn diagrams?

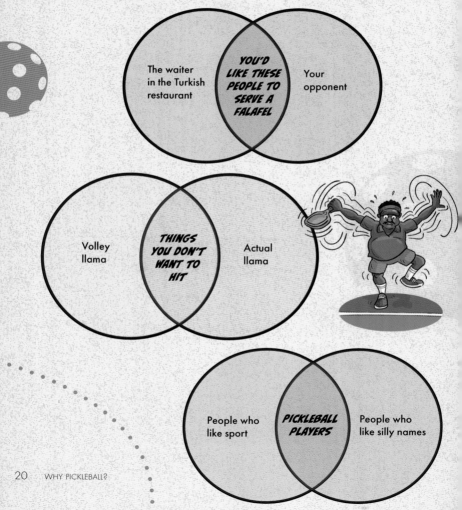

The waiter in the Turkish restaurant

YOU'D LIKE THESE PEOPLE TO SERVE A FALAFEL

Your opponent

Volley llama

THINGS YOU DON'T WANT TO HIT

Actual llama

People who like sport

PICKLEBALL PLAYERS

People who like silly names

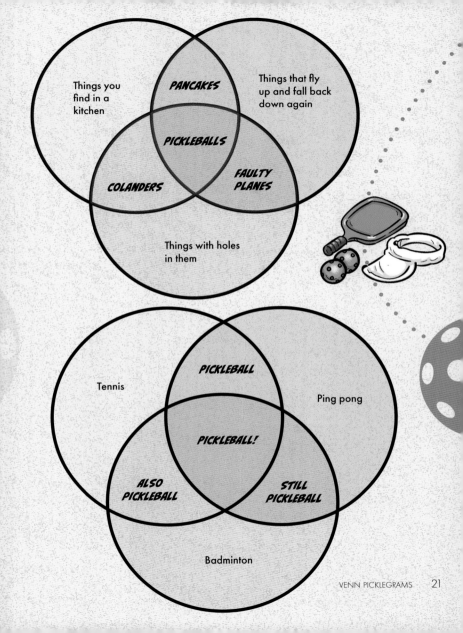

Things you find in a kitchen

PANCAKES

Things that fly up and fall back down again

PICKLEBALLS

COLANDERS

FAULTY PLANES

Things with holes in them

Tennis

PICKLEBALL

Ping pong

PICKLEBALL!

ALSO PICKLEBALL

STILL PICKLEBALL

Badminton

ALL-THE-GEAR, NO-IDEA
Decked out top-to-toe with a head band, knee pads, elbow pads and sweat bands, similar to the tanned ex-pro-golfer and out-of-work actor.

RELUCTANT TEENAGER
Won't move; only plays one-handed; gets annoyed by your enthusiasm; checks phone between points.

THE MANY FACES OF PICKLEBALL

THE RULES ARGUER
He saw it was clearly out, and your Erne shot would never hold up in a court of law!

WIN-AT-ALL-COSTS
Grunting after every shot. Calling every line ball out. Just let them win, there are more important things in life.

RETIRED DENTIST

You're driving it as hard as you can, and they are playing with the calm assurance of a person who's mortgage-free and vacationing in the Seychelles.

ANGRY MUM

The eldest got a tattoo, the vet bill for the cat that hates her was colossal and she hasn't got time for your dinks, spin-drives and sarcasm. She came to pickleball to unwind.

WHICH ONE ARE YOU?

LEAST COMPETITIVE SPORTS PERSON EVER

Why did you partner with someone who applauds everything the opposition does, and is simply 'happy to be in the open air'? Ugh, just get out of my way while I drive this pickle into their face.

JUST·IN·IT·FOR· THE·DRINKS·AFTER

'Let's just call it a draw guys and head to the bar! Three minutes of high-adrenaline sport is enough for anyone!'

TAKE THE PICKLEBALL PERSONALITY TEST

1) YOUR PICKLEBALL PARTNER IS RUNNING LATE. DO YOU...

A) Ditch them. Team up with the 4.0 level player you've had your eye on.

B) Tell them not to sweat it. You'll just hang out on the sidelines and have a chat while you're waiting.

C) Grumble that they should have left work earlier to get here. Don't they realise you both need to work on your third-shot drop?

D) Get some drills under your belt while you're waiting. It's just nice to get out on the court and focus on your serve.

2) A LESS EXPERIENCED PLAYER WANTS TO JOIN YOUR GAME. YOU SAY...

A) Ugh, that's fine, so long as you're on the opposite team. You can demolish them with your backhand punch.

B) Sure! You'd like nothing better! Isn't it great how many people are getting into pickleball these days?

C) Okay, but don't think you're going to go easy on them. You'll have to quiz them on the rules first.

D) Yes, but please don't chat. I'm really in the zone.

3) YOU TRY TO RACE A BALL TO THE BASELINE AND TRIP, TWISTING YOUR KNEE. DO YOU...

A) Get back up and keep playing.
You WILL win this game.

B) Call time and head to the bar. You really should elevate it, and you're sure the bartender has ice...

C) Argue that your opponent landed over the kitchen line when she made that volley, so the point didn't count anyway.

D) Curse your feeble joints and worry that you're going to be out of action for a week. Argh, the torture!

4) YOUR PARTNER CALLS A BALL OUT BUT YOU THINK IT WAS IN. DO YOU...

A) Let it slide. It's to your advantage, and you're sure the opposing team would do the same to you.

B) Call the ball in. It's good sportsmanship, and you're sure the opposition will return the goodwill.

C) Call the ball in, in accordance with rule 6.C.8.

D) Suggest you replay the shot. Who's in a rush? Let's keep enjoying the game.

5) YOU SCORE THE WINNING POINT WITH AN INCREDIBLE CENTRELINE ACE. DO YOU...

A) Whoop and cheer, pumping your fist in the air. You are the CHAMPION!

B) Paddle tap your fellow players. Good game, everyone! Same time next Tuesday?

C) Explain to your partner how they could have made that shot too if they just applied themselves.

D) Replay the glorious moment in your head and resolve to enter that tournament you've been dreaming about.

6) YOUR PALS WANT TO CALL IT A NIGHT AND HEAD TO THE BAR.

A) You tell them they lack discipline and stay behind to do some extra drills.

B) Finally! The bit of the night you've been waiting for.

C) You agree. Once you get a round in, you can point out to them that they repeatedly violated rule 4.E.

D) Is it that time already? Those three hours of pickleball really flew by.

THE RESULTS ARE IN

MOSTLY As

You're in it to win it and you're not going to let anyone stand in your way. You know the rules, but you're not above bending them to your advantage. You pride yourself on your combination of finesse and ferocity and you'll pair up with a partner who is going to help you on your way to glory.

MOSTLY Bs

You're here for a good time, not a long time. Yes, it's fun to get a few games under your belt, but what you love most is the friendly banter, and of course a few drinks at the bar after. Beginner or advanced, you're happy to play with anyone. The more the merrier!

MOSTLY Cs

You've memorised the rule book and you're not going to let anyone forget it. If someone volleys with so much as a toe over the kitchen line, you're going to make sure they know about it. For some reason, you seem to go through partners quicker than you wear out pickleballs – if they can't handle your constructive criticism, that's their problem!

MOSTLY Ds

Ah, pickleball. You love to play out in the fresh air as the sun warms your skin. It's a great work out and a distraction from the pressures of life. You dream of winning the lottery so you can retire and play all day. Singles or doubles? You don't mind, so long as you can get in some really satisfying dinks.

FAMOUS PICKLEHEADS

Pickleball is hitting the bigtime. Everywhere you look, the rich and famous are picking up their paddles and putting a glamorous spin on the sport. Here are some of pickleball's top fans.

SERENA WILLIAMS

She may be the Queen of Tennis, but this Grand Slam GOAT has swapped her strings for a paddle, and loves playing the fun game with her friends and family wherever she goes.

GEORGE AND AMAL CLOONEY

This power couple love the game so much they've built their own pickleball court. They don't play as a team, though – this pair prefers to compete, as playing singles is more of a workout. Clooney has admitted that he often loses to Amal. Maybe Serena could give you some tips, George?

EMMA WATSON

Actor and activist Emma Watson has displayed her love of pickleball in charity tournaments. In the celebrity Pickled tournament, she and boxer Sugar Ray Leonard partnered up as the Volley Ranchers.

> **'IF YOU GON' PICKLE YOU MIGHT AS WELL PICKLE WITH THE BEST!'**
> – Jamie Foxx

JAMIE FOXX

Actor and comedian Jamie Foxx has channelled his pickle passion into his own paddle company, The Best Paddle.

SELENA GOMEZ

She's found fame as a singer and actress, but when she's off the stage she likes nothing better than getting on the pickleball court. Selena Gomez is so passionate about the sport that she's even invested in an LA-based paddle company.

MICHAEL PHELPS

Olympic champion Phelps has emerged from the swimming pool to pick up a paddle. Let's hope he takes off his gold medals first though – they might weigh him down!

BILL GATES

The billionaire tech guru has been dinking for five decades. He can even brag about being one of the first to play the game, since his dad was pals with pickleball creator Joel Pritchard.

> **'I LOVE THAT IT'S EVERYWHERE NOW!'**
> – Serena Williams

10 MORE PICKLEBALL VIPS

Barack Obama
Billie Eilish
Drew Barrymore
Ellen DeGeneres
Justin Bieber
The Kardashians
LeBron James
Leonardo DiCaprio
Owen Wilson
Will Ferrell

HOW TO BRIBE, BEG AND BULLY YOUR PARTNER INTO PLAYING

Pickleball is your new hobby. Your passion. You haven't felt so alive since you discovered Wordle. It's like a switch has been flicked. The birds are singing, the sun is shining, the world is suddenly in technicolour and you want to convert all your friends and family. Their very souls depend on it.

But what's that? Your significant other doesn't realise that the drudgery of their existence could be improved ten thousand-fold if they would only set foot on a pickleball court?! Do not let their indifference deter you. Summon the skills of a world-class preacher and spread the word. Thou shall not rest until the whole world has been converted to the Church of Pickle.

> **'THERE'S NO CATTINESS, THERE'S NO CLIQUISHNESS, THERE'S NONE OF THAT COUNTRY CLUB NONSENSE YOU GET AT A TENNIS CLUB.'**
> – Pro pickler Tyson McGuffin

IRON-CLAD ARGUMENTS TO HELP YOU CONVERT NEW PICKLERS

IT'S SO MUCH FUN – IT DOESN'T MATTER IF YOU WIN OR LOSE!

IT'S AN AMAZING WORKOUT!

JUST GIVE IT A GO – IT'S CHEAPER THAN THERAPY.

DON'T WORRY, IT'S BARELY A WORKOUT.

HOW TO KEEP YOUR OTHER HALF ON THE COURT... WITHOUT HEADING DOWN DIVORCE ALLEY

DON'T try to coach them.
DO float the idea that they get a proper coach. They'll learn faster and they won't want to bite your head off.

DON'T push them to play as partners if they don't want to. They might not be the same skill level.
DO suggest inviting friends to play with you or join a round robin event so you can play in tandem.

DON'T tease them relentlessly that they're too chicken to play you.
DO tell them that you love them so deeply that you want to share this most exquisite of racket sports with them.

'PEOPLE JUST LOVE PICKLEBALL AND THEN ONCE YOU PLAY YOU'RE KINDA HOOKED.'
– Pro pickler Kyle Yates

WHAT'S YOUR PICKLEBALL TEAM NAME?

You've picked your paddle, played a few volleys, and you've found a decent partner. Now all you need is your pickleball team name. Will you go for something witty, pretty, or a moniker that will strike fear into the hearts of your unworthy opponents? If you're short on inspiration, here's a team name generator to do the work for you.

YOUR BIRTH MONTH + YOUR PARTNER'S BIRTH MONTH = YOUR PICKLEBALL TEAM NAME

January	THE PADDLE	January	CRUSHERS
February	THE PICKLE	February	MONSTERS
March	THE DINKING	March	SMASHERS
April	THE KITCHEN	April	OLDIES
May	THE FALAFEL	May	QUEENS
June	THE VOLLEY	June	KINGS
July	THE BACKHAND	July	DIVAS
August	THE COURT	August	CREW
September	THE BLOCK SHOT	September	KILLERS
October	THE ACE	October	DINKS
November	THE TWO-BOUNCE	November	BANGERS
December	THE DILL BALL	December	LLAMAS

The Kitchen Dinks
Dinking Problems
The Big Dills
Made You Dink

Everlasting Lobstoppers
Sets on the Beach
The Ballerinas
The Lobsters

Dill With It
Dispickleballs
Highway Lobbery

PICKLEBALL BINGO

The deeper you fall into the Pickleverse, the more picklers you meet. Shy picklers, wild picklers, picklers that remind you of your favourite grandma, picklers who might just have a shot at going pro. If you can tick off every pickle type on this bingo card, shout PICKLE!

PLAYER WITH MORE THAN 6 PADDLES	PLAYER WHO LIKES TO DROP THEIR RATING INTO CONVERSATION
PLAYER WHO TRIES TO CONVERT EVERYONE TO PICKLEBALL	PLAYER WHO HAS TRAVELLED TO A TOURNAMENT
PLAYER WHO LOVES A CROSS-COURT DINK	PLAYER WHO WATCHES PICKLEBALL YOUTUBE VIDEOS
PLAYER WITH A STRONG BACKHAND	PLAYER WHO IS UNDER 20
PLAYER WHO RETIRED EARLY TO FIT IN MORE PICKLEBALL	PLAYER WHO IS A BANGER

PLAYER WHO IS ALWAYS INJURED

PLAYER WHO ALWAYS ARGUES THE LINE CALL

PLAYER WHO WEARS PICKLEBALL SLOGAN T-SHIRTS

PLAYER WHO IS LEFT-HANDED

PLAYER WHO CAN'T RESIST A PICKLEBALL PUN

PLAYER WHO HATES HAVING TO SHARE A COURT WITH BEGINNERS

PLAYER WHO 'GOT INTO PICKLEBALL BEFORE IT WAS POPULAR'

PLAYER WHO ALWAYS HAS THE LATEST EQUIPMENT

PLAYER WHO LOVES A DINK FAKE

PLAYER WHO USED TO PLAY TENNIS

PLAYER WHO IS OVER 75

PLAYER WHO IS EVERYONE'S CHEERLEADER

PLAYER WHO IS TRYING TO MASTER THE CHAINSAW SERVE

PLAYER WHO CAN RECITE THE RULE BOOK

PLAYER WHO SENDS YOU PICKLEBALL MEMES

HATERS GONNA HATE

It's time for the cold, hard truth. This is a twisted, messed-up world full of twisted, messed-up people. A world in which a tiny, deluded minority – whisper it – don't like pickleball.

As devastating as that news must be, you're going to have to hold your head high, turn the other cheek, and keep on pickling. Life is too short and the dinks are too sweet to worry about what others think.

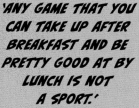

WHAT THE HATERS SAY

'NOT AS FUN AS PING PONG. NOT AS ELEGANT AS TENNIS. NOT AS PRETTY AS GOLF.'

– Sportswriter Rick Reilly, *The Washington Post*

'MORE OF A HOBBY THAN A SPORT—IT'S A FIDGET SPINNER THAT REQUIRES MORE WORK.'

– Podcaster and pickleball sceptic **Chris Black**

'A GYM-CLASS GAME THAT SHOULD COME WITH A MANDATORY VASECTOMY FOR EVERY ADULT MALE WHO PLAYS IT.'

– Brian Moylan, *New York Vulture*

'ANY GAME THAT YOU CAN TAKE UP AFTER BREAKFAST AND BE PRETTY GOOD AT BY LUNCH IS NOT A SPORT.'

– Sportswriter Rick Reilly, *The Washington Post*

WHY DON'T PEOPLE LIKE PICKLEBALL?

- The loud, annoying pwock noise – people have moved house to get away from it.

- Tennis courts are being converted into pickleball courts, and that makes the tennis players furious.

- Because of its stratospheric rise in popularity – it seems like everyone's talking about it.

- Sports fans (particularly tennis buffs) think the game is boring to watch.

- They think it has a stupid name.

WHAT CAN YOU DO ABOUT IT?

- Challenge the nay-sayers to a game. They think it doesn't require much movement? Try it. They think it doesn't require skill? Let's see them try to beat you. It might be easier to learn than tennis, but that doesn't mean it's easier to win.

- Laugh it off. If they're so bored by picklers talking pickleball, why are they adding to the conversation?

- Pity them. Like school bullies, those sad, deluded haters are really just jealous you're having so much pickling good fun.

- Keep on pickling. Haters gonna hate.

ALTERNATIVE NAMES FOR PICKLEBALL

Pickleball. Some love the name, some hate it. Some thought they hated it, but then they got sucked in to the sweet, sweet game and now they worship at the Alter of the Pickle Gods. But if playing a sport that could be preserved in a jar of vinegar leaves a sour taste in your mouth, you better come up with your own nickname. Here are some alternatives that may or may not turn your stomach.

- **MURDER BAT** (Not to be confused with those fluttering vampires of the night)

- **PASSIVE-AGGRESSIVE BATTERS** (Self-depreciating)

- **POWERBALL** (Hmm... isn't that something to do with the lottery?)

- **PWOCKBALL** (That's right. We're owning that headache-inducing noise pollution)

CHANNEL YOUR INNER HAWAIIAN AND CALL IT PUKABALL (MEANING 'HOLE BALL'), AS THEY DO IN THE ALOHA STATE.

. . . .

> 'I THINK IT WOULD BE A LOT EASIER TO CONVINCE PEOPLE TO PLAY THE SPORT IF IT WASN'T SUCH A SILLY NAME.'
> – Pro pickler Ben Johns

IF YOU THOUGHT THE GAME WAS CALLED PICK-A-BALL OR PRICKLEBALL, MAYBE GET YOUR EARS CLEANED.

- **WIFFLE TENNIS** (It's not really a wiffle ball. It's not really tennis. Not fun, not memorable, but at least there isn't a dill pickle in sight.)

- **DOMINATION BALL** (Don't you mess with us, Djokovic!)

Not keen on any of these options either? What do *you* think the sport should be called?

Is pickleball really such a weird name anyway? What about ping pong? You can't get much sillier than that. Take a cold hard look at yourself. If you're too fancy to say the name 'pickleball' out loud, maybe you shouldn't be playing it. Pull that paddle out of your butt or get off our court.

'WHO CARES WHAT IT'S CALLED?'
– Pro pickler Kyle Yates

OI, THAT'S NOT PICKLEBALL!

Okay, take a deep breath and calm down. No one doubts your dedication to pickleball. Nevertheless, you're going to have to accept that it does have competition. It turns out there are one or two people out there who — brace yourself — like another paddle sport better. So, what are these sordid games that have ensnared innocent sports enthusiasts across the globe?

POP TENNIS

Since its genesis in Michigan in 1898, this sport has gone through a few names. First paddle tennis, then California paddle, and now POP, short for 'popular'. That might be a misnomer, since its popularity has waxed and waned, and it's never really taken off outside the U.S. But, with nearly two million players, perhaps it's just biding its time. With tennis scoring, a softer ball, and a court less than half the size of a tennis court, it's a great beginner's sport.

PLATFORM TENNIS

For those who don't want freezing temperatures getting in the way of their paddle sports, there's the quirky nephew of POP: platform tennis. Invented in New York in 1928, it has a similar court size to pickleball, but surrounded by wire fences. Why is it called platform tennis? It's played on a raised, heated platform, to keep it off the uneven, snowy ground.

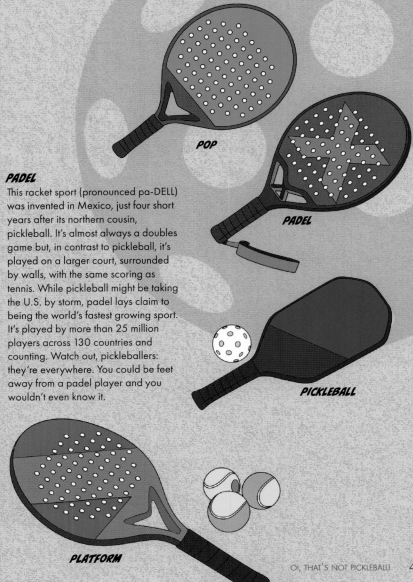

POP

PADEL

PICKLEBALL

PLATFORM

PADEL

This racket sport (pronounced pa-DELL) was invented in Mexico, just four short years after its northern cousin, pickleball. It's almost always a doubles game but, in contrast to pickleball, it's played on a larger court, surrounded by walls, with the same scoring as tennis. While pickleball might be taking the U.S. by storm, padel lays claim to being the world's fastest growing sport. It's played by more than 25 million players across 130 countries and counting. Watch out, pickleballers: they're everywhere. You could be feet away from a padel player and you wouldn't even know it.

'ONE OF THE THINGS ABOUT PICKLEBALL IS THAT THE LEARNING CURVE IS VERY QUICK.'

– Pro pickler Tyson McGuffin

CHAPTER THREE

THE ART OF PICKLEBALL

It's a well-known adage that pickleball is easy to learn but difficult to master. You start out as a bashful newbie, spouting pickling terms and trying not to drop your paddle, but with perseverance bordering on obsession, you might just make it to tournament level. Whether you're a 1.0 or a 4.5, here's a rundown of the rules, shots and silly lingo that make pickleball the sport that gets everyone hooked.

LOOKING GOOD FOR THE GAME IS HALF THE BATTLE

Sure, you could slope up to the pickleball court in your faded shorts and your t-shirt with questionable stains. What do you have to prove? Be careful, though – you'll risk making your partner cringe so hard they give themselves a stitch before they even set foot in the kitchen. Instead, don't miss this chance to impress. Wow your competitors with threads as smart as your backhand spins and show them that even fashionistas have the skills to win.

SHOES

To get the best out of your game, choose a lightweight shoe with good grip, cushioning and lateral support. You can now find trainers specifically designed for pickleball, but tennis shoes will do the job. Unless you're hitting the courts several times a week, you might not need bleeding-edge shoe technology but, for the love of pickle, make sure your footwear has proper tread. No one wants to see you doing the splits for the first time in 40 years.

OUTFIT

Pickleball is the young maverick of racket sports. While tennis players are busy bleaching their Wimbledon whites, picklers are picking out their next eye-catching outfit. Don't be afraid to let your personality shine with bright colours and bold patterns. Just make sure your clothing's got you covered – you don't want to be arrested for indecent exposure every time you bend down to grab the ball.

IF YOU'RE PLAYING ON AN INDOOR COURT, CHOOSE SHOES WITH NON-MARKING SOLES.

CHOOSE CLOTHING THAT...
- Keeps you cool
- Wicks away moisture
- Allows maximum movement
- Has pockets or a cheeky spot to tuck away an extra ball

IF YOU'RE PLAYING IN A TOURNAMENT, YOU CAN'T WEAR A COLOUR THAT MATCHES THE BALL. THAT'S A WORSE FAUX PAS THAN A WEDDING GUEST IN A WHITE DRESS.

WHAT THE COLOUR OF YOUR SWEATBANDS SAY ABOUT YOU

RED – 'Don't mess with me. I'm in it to win it and I will OBLITERATE YOU.'

ORANGE – 'I can play nine straight hours of pickleball fuelled only by energy drinks and the buzz of the game!'

YELLOW – 'The sun is shining, the paddles are swinging and soon we'll be at the bar sipping our post-pickle cocktails.'

GREEN – 'I'm so chill, I could dink that ball into your court without moving my paddle.'

BLUE – 'I'm just trying this out because TikTok told me that the Kardashians played.'

PURPLE – 'Don't even dare suggest you love pickleball more than I do. Pickleball is a fundamental aspect of my personality and without it I will crumble!'

WHITE – 'I'm really more of a tennis player. But this is fun too, I guess.'

PIMP THAT PADDLE

Every pickleball player needs a paddle, but which type you choose depends on your style and experience level. You might start off with a basic model and tell yourself 'This'll do me fine', but before you know it you'll be lusting after the latest model that promises to make your dinks that little bit dinkier, your lobs more luxuriously lobby, and your teammate just a teeny, tiny bit jealous...

YOU WANT IT... BUT DO YOU NEED IT?

With around 600 companies competing to sell you the next cutting-edge paddle, take a good, hard look into your soul and ask yourself this: what would really improve your game? Spending a day's salary on a new paddle, or losing a few inches off your waistline?

MY PRECIOUSSSSS

THE GOLDILOCKS PADDLE

Try out different paddles to find the one that suits you best.
Look out for:

GRIP – you don't want your paddle to be flying out of your hand as soon as you break a sweat.

WEIGHT – a top-of-the-range paddle is no good if it'll strain your wrist just to swing it.

POWER – if you're a banger, you'll need a paddle that can pack some punch.

CONTROL – if your game is all about finesse, make sure your paddle gives you plenty of control. Most players will want a combination of power and control.

PADDLE TIP

On open play courts (where there are no bookings and anyone can turn up), players often keep their place in line by adding their paddle to a rack – once your paddle is at the front of the queue, it's your turn to play. To keep track of which paddle is yours, make sure your name is on it. It makes life so much easier.

THE BALL'S IN YOUR COURT

Rookie players, here's your chance to bone up on the pickleball court. If you're used to lunging across the vast expanse of a tennis court, the comparatively puny pickleball court will seem like a walk in the park. Don't get cocky, though — one wrong move in the kitchen and your opponents will have the upper hand.

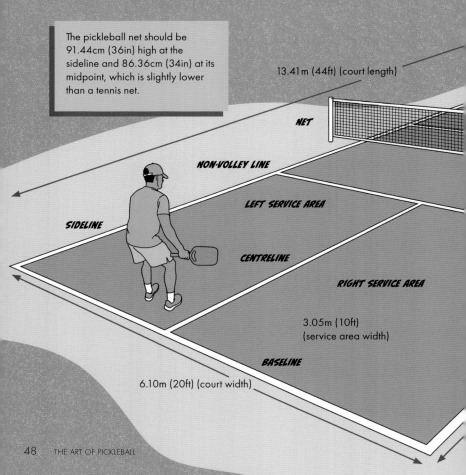

The pickleball net should be 91.44cm (36in) high at the sideline and 86.36cm (34in) at its midpoint, which is slightly lower than a tennis net.

13.41m (44ft) (court length)

NET

NON-VOLLEY LINE

LEFT SERVICE AREA

CENTRELINE

RIGHT SERVICE AREA

3.05m (10ft) (service area width)

SIDELINE

BASELINE

6.10m (20ft) (court width)

At less than half the surface area, a pickleball court is much smaller than its older cousin, the tennis court. This makes it a popular option for anyone tight on space. (Not that tight on space, though. Let's face it – you're never going to fit it into a studio apartment.)

MATERIAL DIFFERENCE

With pickleball, pretty much any surface goes. While tournament level courts use a special polyurethane sports surface, outdoor courts can be concrete, clay, asphalt, astroturf or grass.

CONCRETE – this durable surface will give you a fast, hard game. Not so great for your poor old joints though and, if you fall, you're sure as hell going to feel it.

ASPHALT – has more bounce than concrete, so it has better shock absorption. It should also give you a decent grip, helping you avoid any spectacular slides.

CLAY – clay courts are fast gaining popularity in the pickleball community. They're lower impact than playing on a hard court, producing a slower game and a less regular bounce.

GRASS – this surface provides a challenge to players as it needs to be rock-hard so that the ball bounces enough. Otherwise, matches can be over VERY quickly!

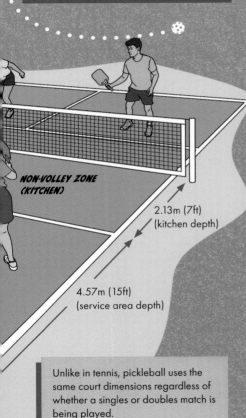

NON-VOLLEY ZONE (KITCHEN)

2.13m (7ft) (kitchen depth)

4.57m (15ft) (service area depth)

Unlike in tennis, pickleball uses the same court dimensions regardless of whether a singles or doubles match is being played.

FOR THOSE WHO ARE ABOUT TO PICKLE

One of pickleball's many strengths is the ease with which new players can pick up the rules. But before anyone throws a tantrum over a wrong line call or a fumbled serve, here's a summary of the sport's basic rules.

SERVING
- The serve must be underhand. The paddle must make contact with the ball while below the bellybutton.
- The server must keep at least one of their feet behind the baseline and within the side line.
- The server must hit the ball diagonally across the net into the opponent's service court.

THE TWO-BOUNCE RULE
- After the ball has been served, the receiving team must let the ball bounce once before they return it.
- The serving team must then also let the ball bounce once before their return shot.
- After this, players can choose to hit the ball before or after it bounces. (Hitting the ball before it's had a chance to bounce is a volley.)

THE NON-VOLLEY ZONE (KITCHEN)
- Volleys are only allowed after the second shot. When hitting a volley, the player must keep their feet behind the non-volley zone.

WINNING POINTS
- Only the serving team can score points. They do so when the opposing team commits a fault. If the serving team commits a fault, the rally ends and the serve switches to the other team.

IS THIS TOO HIGH?

COMMON PICKLEBALL FAULTS
- You hit the ball into the net.
- You hit the ball out of bounds.
- You volley the ball before the third shot.
- You volley the ball from within the non-volley zone.
- You allow the ball to bounce twice on the same side of the net.

DEAD BALL - A BALL THAT IS NO LONGER IN PLAY, OR AN ACTION THAT STOPS PLAY.

YEAH, I'D SAY THAT BALL'S OUT.

SCORING

If you're new to pickleball, then the scoring system can seem confusing at first. But, after a game or two, it's easy to keep track.

Unlike in other racket sports, in pickleball, only the serving team can score points. They win a point every time the non-serving team, or singles player, commits a fault.

When the serving team's score is even (0, 2, 4, etc), the player who served first in the game will be in the right (even) side of the court. When the score is odd (1, 3, 5, etc), they will be in the left (odd) side of the court.

CALLING THE SCORE

A pickleball score is called before each serve. In singles, the score is just two numbers, but in doubles matches, it is called as three numbers.

1ST NUMBER = server's score

2ND NUMBER = receiver's score

3RD NUMBER = the server number (1 or 2)

AT THE BEGINNING OF A DOUBLE'S MATCH, THE SCORE IS CALLED AS 0 - 0 - 2

SETTLING THE SCORE

Some pickleballers think that the scoring system should change. They want the sport to adopt rally scoring, where a point is won by either team at the end of each rally, the same as in many other racket sports. Others disagree – they think this will make the game more about attack than defence, making it more like tennis. For this young sport, only time will tell which scoring system will win out.

THE PLAYER WHO SERVES FIRST IN THE GAME IS CALLED SERVER NUMBER 2.

THE UNWRITTEN RULES

There is more to playing pickleball than just following the rule book. That will tell you what counts as a fault, how to make the right line call and when to call the score, but it doesn't lay out all the rules for how to behave. Here's what you need to know to make sure everyone playing on the courts has a good time and – more importantly – stays safe.

1.

Don't lob stray balls back across several courts. Locate its owner, wait for a safe moment, and roll it back to them.

2.

If your ball goes onto someone else's court, call out **'Ball on court!'** to let them know. You don't want a rogue ball to ruin their game.

3.

Don't steal balls. If a ball strays onto your court, return it... even if it looks all new and pretty.

4.

Wait before you walk. Don't just wander across the courts like you own the place (even if it's your own personal pickleball court and you do, in fact, own the place). It can be dangerous and it's definitely annoying. Wait until there is a pause in play, make sure the players know you're about to cross, and then walk. **No dawdling**.

5.

As much as you may feel like channelling your inner John McEnroe, remember: you are a pickler, not an 80s tennis icon. **Don't throw your paddle** or use bad language.

6.

If you're playing on open courts, join the queuing system and **don't jump your place**. If you're not sure what the system is, ask another player.

8.

Don't want anyone crushing your designer shades? Check the court surface and **clear up after yourself** when you're done.

7.

In the adulterated words of Geoffrey Chaucer, time and tide and an empty pickleball court wait for no man. **Make sure you're ready** to play when it's your turn.

ANYONE FOR A GAME?

VITAL VERNACULAR

Any self-respecting pickler knows their dill balls from their dairy queens and their flapjacks from their falafels. Learn the lingo so you can talk like you're a pro, even when you've been pickled.

ACE

Just like in tennis, this is a serve that your opponent fails to return, giving you a point.

BAGEL

A game that's been won 11-0, with the losing team winning no points.

BANGER

A player who likes to hit the ball hard in order to overpower their opponents. Thwack!

BASH

A hard shot that has – usually by accident – hit the top of the net before landing on the opponent's side of the court. It's normally very tricky to return the ball after this sort of shot.

BERT

A shot in which the player runs in front of their partner to hit an Erne on the partner's side of the court.

CHICKEN WING

The position of a player's paddle arm where their elbow points up and their paddle points down (like a chicken wing), as they try to hit a ball coming straight towards their armpit on their paddle side.

DAIRY QUEEN

Just like the ice cream, this is a soft serve.

DEAD BALL

A ball that is no longer in play, or an action that stops play.

DILL BALL

A ball that has bounced once legally on the opponent's side and is in play.

DINK

You'll want to master this classic return shot, where the ball is hit softly at, inside or near your kitchen line into the opposition's non-volley zone, just clearing the net and giving them little chance to return.

DIVORCE ALLEY

The area between two partners where each player may think the other one might hit the ball, and so hesitate in taking the shot. This makes it an appealing place for their opponents to aim the ball.

ERNE

An advanced shot named after pickleballer Erne Perry, in which the player hits the ball in the air while jumping around the kitchen or with their feet positioned outside of the court (in the pantry). This move allows them to hit the ball close to the net without entering the kitchen.

FALAFEL

This is the rather inglorious term for a shot that falls short because it's been miss-hit or hit too softly. Like if you tried to hit a falafel instead of a pickleball. Bleurgh.

FLAPJACK

A shot that must be allowed to bounce before being hit.

GOLDEN PICKLE

As heavenly as it sounds. This is a perfect game in pickleball, achieved when the first team serving wins the game using only its first server. The losing team never even gets to serve, let alone win a point. They're never allowed to forget it, either...

HINDER

Any event or object that affects play, such as another ball or a person walking across the court. If a hinder, or hindrance, occurs, a dead ball is called and the point is replayed.

KITCHEN

No, this isn't where everyone hangs out at the after-match party. The kitchen is the non-volley zone (NVZ).

NASTY NELSON

If you want to play dirty, pull a Nasty Nelson. In this seldom-used serve, the server intentionally hits the non-receiving player with the ball – if they are near the net and the centreline – to gain a point. Don't expect your opponents to buy you a drink after, though.

NO MAN'S LAND

Also known as the transition area or zone, this is the part of the court midway between the kitchen line and the baseline. It's a risky place to be standing, so get moving.

PADDLE TAP

Tapping the butt of your paddle's handle against another player's is the sporting way to say 'good game' to your fellow picklers at the end of a game. After all, they don't need to see you're secretly fuming inside.

PANTRY

The area outside of the court on either side of the kitchen.

PICKLED

If you lose a game without scoring a point, you've been pickled. It happens to the best of us. Dust yourself off and ask for the best of three.

PICKLEDOME

The main court where a championship match is played. Dream big – one day you might find yourself strutting your stuff on the pickledome.

PICKLEHEAD

A fan of pickleball, also known as a pickler.

POACHER

A player who frequently crosses the centreline to intercept shots that were intended for their partner. Not cool, dude. Not cool.

SHADOWING

Moving in sync with your partner, around 3m (10ft) apart, in order to keep a consistent distance between you as you approach or retreat from the net.

SMASH

A powerful over-arm shot hit from above the player's head, also known as an 'overhead', but let's face it, that doesn't sound as fun.

SOFT GAME

A game that focuses on skill and dexterity rather than brute strength, usually employing plenty of clever dinks and drop shots.

TAGGING

Hitting an opponent on purpose to win a point. Ouch! Does your mother know you play like that?

TWEENER

This is when a player returns a shot by hitting the ball between their own legs. Yes, it can look magnificent. But if you flunk it, you're going to look like an idiot.

VOLLEY LLAMA

When a player illegally volleys the ball while their feet are in the kitchen. It's called the non-volley zone for a reason. FAULT!

11 WAYS TO DEAL WITH ARGUMENTS

Most pickleball games won't have a referee officiating, so it's vital that the players play with fairness and integrity. Even so, there are bound to be times when players disagree. If that happens, here are some strategies to help you keep the game running smoothly.

1.

Firstly, remember that **the rulebook is clear**: you make the call about the ball when it's on your side of the net. If you see the ball bounce outside the line, but your opponent argues that it's in, you still have the right to call it out. Be firm but polite.

2.

Likewise, when the ball is on your opponent's side, it's their call to make. If you disagree, it's still best to give them the benefit of the doubt. **Think long and hard before you pick an argument.**

3.

If you have any doubt as to whether a ball was in or out, you should make the call in your opponent's favour. Even if you have to whisper a calming mantra to yourself while you do so.

4.

If you and your partner disagree about a line call or a fault, you can ask your opponents' opinion. Once you do this, though, you must go with their judgement. **Hold in that rant** like you hold in a fart when you're at your in-laws'.

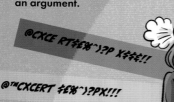

5.

If you and your opponents can't agree on a call, **you could offer to replay the point**. Be careful not to overuse this option, though. It's better just to trust that each player is making the most accurate calls they can and that it will all balance out in the end. Constant replays can get frustrating and spoil the flow of the game.

6.

If you and your opponent still can't see eye-to-eye, **be the bigger person**. Let them have the point and move on. If this becomes a regular occurrence, think carefully about whether you want to play them again.

7.

If you're playing in a tournament, you could call a referee over to arbitrate. Keep calm and don't take your frustration out on them – that is not going to win you any extra points.

8.

If a player calls a rule violation that you don't agree with, stay calm and discuss the rule with them after the game. You may have both interpreted the rule book differently. If it still rankles, take it up with your therapist.

9.

If all else fails, you could play **Rock, Paper, Scissors**.

10.

Bite your tongue and then go and rant on the Internet. That's what it was invented for, wasn't it?

11.

Last but not least, take a deep breath, remind yourself that it's just a game, and suggest you all go and get yourselves a snack. **No one makes good decisions when they're hangry**.

7 EXCUSES TO GET YOU OUT OF THE OFFICE AND ONTO THE COURT

We get it. You're a responsible adult. You're dedicated to your career. But sometimes the pull of the pickleball court is just too strong. Squash your morals deep down inside you and do whatever it takes to ditch your job and head to the net.

EXCUSE: 'I think there was something wrong with my lunch – my stomach doesn't feel good.'

TRANSLATION: I've timed my lunch superbly to give me just the right level of nutrients and energy for a perfect pickleball game at 3 o'clock.

EXCUSE: 'I'm so sorry, my brother is having a crisis and I need to be there to support him.'

TRANSLATION: His crisis is that he needs a pickleball partner! I'll be supporting him with a clever cross-court dink and a wicked backhand punch.

EXCUSE: 'I'm going to be late in today, I'm afraid. The school has just rung to say my children have nits and now I'm itching like crazy. Must treat it urgently!'

TRANSLATION: I do have an itch I need to scratch. A pickleball itch. See you later, suckers!

EXCUSE: 'I've got to leave early for a doctor's appointment today. I'd say what it's for... but it's a bit embarrassing.'

TRANSLATION: I've bagged myself a 1:1 training session with a top coach. I'm hoping they can cure my embarrassingly bad backhand.

EXCUSE: 'I'm sorry, my dad just called. He's injured his knee and really needs my help.'

TRANSLATION: He did injure his knee – last Tuesday. He needs me to stand in for him in a pickleball game.

EXCUSE: 'Ugh, I know this is gross, but I've woken up today with the worst D&V. There's no way I can make it in.'

TRANSLATION: I DO have the worst D&V... if by that you mean dinking and volleying.

EXCUSE: 'I'm going to be late in. My car won't start so I need to get a mechanic out to look at it.'

TRANSLATION: My car won't start because I'm down at the courts for a spot of early morning pickleball. I imagine it will miraculously fix itself in an hour or two.

INDOOR VS OUTDOOR: WHICH TRIBE ARE YOU?

TEAM OUTDOOR

- Breathe in that fresh air!
- Feel the wind in your hair!
- The chance of rain is a small price to pay.
- The wind might blow the ball off course? The added challenge is half the fun!
- All that Vitamin D gives me a boost.
- When the sun goes down, we'll turn on the floodlights.
- You can hear your partner on an outdoor court. It's so noisy indoors, you can't even hear yourself think.

TEAM INDOOR

- Bad weather isn't going to stop me playing pickleball.
- Sunburn? Heatstroke? No thank you.
- Who needs daylight? Not us. It'll only make you squint when the sun's in your eyes.
- The extra noise is a small price to pay for the comfort of central heating.
- There's no breeze to contend with here. Nothing's going to send my shot off course... except my poor aim.

A CHANGE OF PACE

On an outdoor court, the harder balls bounce more, giving them more power and making it easier to reach for volleys, but a faster pace of play. On an indoor court, the lighter balls can't be hit with as much power, leading to longer rallies.

SCRATCHING THE SURFACE

Some indoor courts use the same sports surface as outdoor courts, but in others you might find yourself playing on wood. The different surface is going to change your game just as much as environmental factors. On the plus side, wood and specialized sports surfaces are easier on a player's joints than playing on concrete.

A WHIFF OF THE WIFFLE

With its distinctive pop sound as it smacks down on the court, the hollow plastic pickleball is already an iconic piece of sporting equipment. Yes, it may look like a cat toy, but this little ball can inspire joy and rage in equal measure. The very first ball used to play pickle may have been a wiffle ball, but these days pickleballs are in a league of their own. Outdoor pickleballs are harder, heavier and have smaller holes to cope with wind, while indoor balls are lighter with bigger holes. Make sure you pick the right ones for your game.

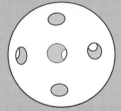

Indoor – 26 larger holes

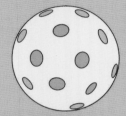

Outdoor – 40 smaller holes

NO CLEAR WINNER

Indoor and outdoor both have their devotees, but ultimately it comes down to the weather. If you live in balmy California, there's a good chance you're going to be able to put in the hours on an outdoor pickleball court. If you've caught the pickleball bug in wet and windy Scotland, you might be better off booking an indoor court. Even so, many players in northern climes play outdoors all year round. If you don't mind shovelling a bit of snow then, by all means, play on!

IDEAL PICKLEBALLER DIET VS ACTUAL PICKLEBALLER DIET

If you're a dedicated pickleballer pushing yourself towards your next tournament, you're probably taking your diet seriously, trying to boost your performance with perfectly balanced nutrition. As for the rest of us? Well, we might have ambitious New Year's resolutions, but by the time the pickleball cocktails appear in summer, there's a good chance our will power is faltering like a ball grazing the net.

THE IDEAL DIET

- Carbohydrates for energy. Think wholegrains, fruits and vegetables. For a quick pre-match snack, bananas are a wonderfood full of carbs and potassium.
- Protein to build muscle. Lean meat, fish, eggs, tofu, beans and nuts are your friends.
- Hydration for functioning and focus. You can't beat plain old water.

THE REAL DIET

- Leftovers from the night before – who has time to cook when there's pickleball to be played?
- A Friday night takeaway with your pickleball buddies. All play and no food make Jack a hungry boy.
- Sports drinks to give you a boost. Mmm, feel that sugary goodness coursing through your veins! Who's up for another game?
- A cocktail to celebrate a great session. Did someone say happy hour?

MAKE SURE YOU ARE FULLY HYDRATED BEFORE YOU BEGIN A GAME. THIS IS ESPECIALLY IMPORTANT IF YOU'RE PLAYING OUTSIDE ON A HOT DAY. FAINTING ON COURT ISN'T A GREAT LOOK.

> 'I EAT WHAT I LIKE TO EAT, BUT USUALLY NOT TOO MUCH OF IT ... DURING TOURNAMENTS IT'S USUALLY NUTS, FRUIT, AND LOTS OF COCONUT WATER.'
>
> – Pro pickleballer Simone Jardim on tournament snacks

PLANNING AHEAD

For peak performance, eat a meal three to four hours before a match. Avoid very fatty and protein-heavy foods, as they take longer for your digestive system to process and could make you feel sluggish.

THE HEALTHY SNACK CHECKLIST

If the mere thought of ditching processed snacks makes your energy levels dip, try nibbling on these more wholesome options next time you're heading for the court.

- Cashews
- Pistachios
- Almonds
- Pumpkin seeds
- Raisins
- Dried cranberries
- Dates
- Apples
- Bananas
- Grapes

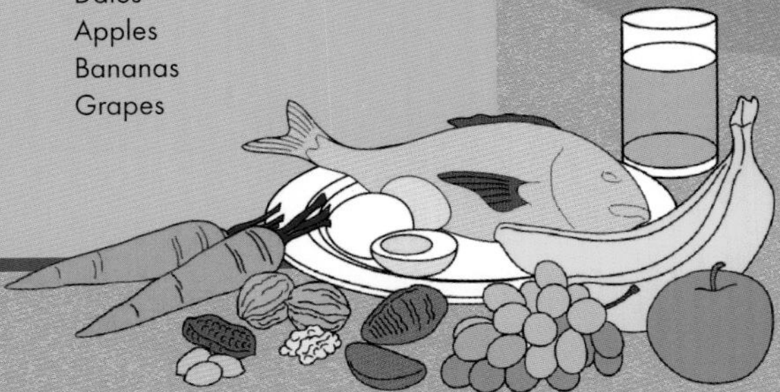

THE PICKLER'S ARMOURY

Whether you fancy yourself as the embodiment of finesse or a banger who's going to dominate through sheer power, you need to get to grips with the basic strokes used on the pickleball court. A stroke is the way in which you hit the ball. Think of them like the essential building blocks, out of which you build a successful match.

GROUNDSTROKE

No, this isn't some weird asphalt fetish where you lie down and caress the court surface. It's the catch-all term for any shot made after the ball has bounced once. So, really, almost all shots are groundstrokes.

DINK

The cutest but cruellest of strokes, and a signature move in pickleball. The dink is a near-net stroke of gentle elegance played with a smooth upward movement that pops the ball over the net into the kitchen, taking all the power off the shot. To achieve the perfect dink stroke, you need to hit the ball as softly and with as much precision as you can. Play to your opponent's weaker side (forehand or backhand?) and make the angle as acute as possible.

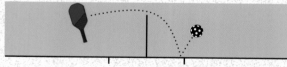

ALWAYS DINK FROM IN FRONT OF YOUR BODY.

BE CAREFUL NOT TO PUT SO MUCH JUICE INTO YOUR VOLLEY THAT IT GOES OUT OF BOUNDS.

THINK YOU CAN BEAT ME, DO YOU?!

VOLLEY

Just like in tennis, a volley is any shot that is made before the ball has hit the ground. While a dink is all about skill, a volley is often more powerful. Just don't get carried away and volley in the kitchen. Don't volley in your actual kitchen either – your partner won't be impressed with your overhead smash if you smash all the dishes while you're at it.

ALL HAIL THE DINK! – A regulation dink will rarely win a point (unless you've engineered your opponent hopelessly out of position), but it will take the sting out of rallies and make things awkward for your adversary. Any point won with a dink should be celebrated fully with high fives and chest bumps! Nothing hurts the opposition more than a dinked defeat.

SNEAKY SOFT SHOTS

If you can't match your opponent on strength and speed, outmanoeuvre them with cleverly placed shots that keep them guessing. But watch out — these shots require patience and precision.

> 'YOU CAN BE AS ATHLETIC AS YOU WANT ... BUT YOU DON'T HAVE TO BE IN ORDER TO BE GOOD.'
> — Pro pickler Ben Johns

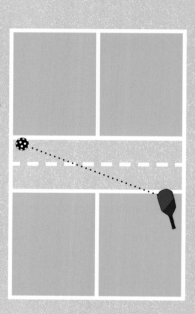

CROSS-COURT DINK

The clue is in the name with this clever dink. You hit the shot from one side of the court, across to your opponent's other side. Unlike a down-the-line dink, this one needs a bit more power to get it across the longer diagonal distance. It's a tricky shot to pull off but can be extremely effective once you have the knack.

MORE DINKS THAN YOU THINK

Think you've got the dink down? Dink again! There's the push dink, the topspin dink, the slice dink. You can dink forehand or backhand. If you want to be a master pickler, you're going to have to become one with your paddle and perfect every shot.

WHEN DINKING, KEEP YOUR WRIST STIFF AND USE YOUR SHOULDER.

SHORT-HOP DINK

This is an excellent shot choice for when you need to hit a low ball. Hit the ball just after it's bounced when it is still close to the ground. This will let you stay near the kitchen line rather than having to step backwards to hit the shot when the ball is higher in the air, giving your opponent less time to prepare for their next shot.

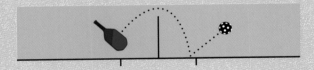

THIRD-SHOT DROP

This is a difficult and pivotal shot, and one you'll need to master if you want to progress up the ratings. As the name suggests, this is the third shot after the serve, and that means it's the first shot after the two-shot rule. It's likely your opponents will already be at the kitchen line, while you're still at the baseline.

Hitting a drop shot at this point will send the ball in a high arc, landing softly in the kitchen and forcing your opponent to dink it back to you instead of whacking a powerful volley. Meanwhile, you'll have vital seconds to cover the ground from the baseline to the kitchen.

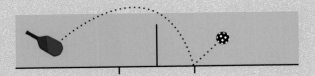

PUNCHY POWER SHOTS

Just because you've mastered the soft shots, doesn't mean you can't add some power to your game. Let off a little steam with these satisfyingly forceful shots and watch as your opponents scramble to keep up.

LOB

To hit a lob shot, you'll need to send the ball high over your opponents' heads, forcing them to turn around and run to the baseline to return the shot. It can be a clever shot to keep up your sleeve if your opponent is smashing the ball back at you quicker than you can catch your breath. Done right, it allows you to take back control.

TO DRIVE THE BALL HARD, START WITH A WIDE, SQUARE STANCE AND BENT KNEES.

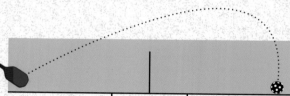

THE DRIVE

Hard, fast and often unstoppable – this is your superpower. It's a volley or ground shot hit as hard as you can. Use it sparingly, as you don't want to be predictable, but let them know it's in your armoury – the intimidation factor will be huge! Drive the pickle at a charging opponent or a vacant area of the court. A driven winner is a statement that you're a pickler of precision and power.

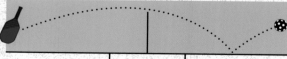

OVERHEAD SMASH

Glorious, definitive and game-winning, an overhead smash is the same as in tennis and badminton in its style and devastation. Hold your bat high and rake downwards as hard as you can manage.

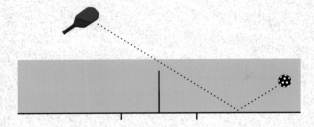

BACKHAND PUNCH VOLLEY

The punch volley is an excellent weapon to add to your pickleball arsenal. Bring out this shot when you're near the net, punching the ball with a compact motion, speeding it back towards your opponent. Whether they are trying to quicken the pace, or they've sent you a gentle dink, this quick backhand move has the element of surprise.

TWO-HANDED BACKHAND

Putting your non-dominant hand on the back of your paddle helps add stability and power to your backhand shot, turning a defensive move into an offensive attack.

'IT'S A POWER SHOT THAT CAN BE HIT BEHIND YOU. IT'S GOOD FOR COUNTERING.'

– Pro pickler Callie Jo Smith on the two-handed backhand

DEVILISH DEFENCES

Don't let your opponents take control of the game. Whether they're coming at you hard or playing a soft game, be ready with defensive moves to take on any shot they send your way.

THE BLOCK

'You drive me and I'll block you buddy!' The block shot is your friend. Simply get your paddle in the way and let it hit. It'll slow the game down if it's all getting a bit feisty! Using your backhand, hold the paddle in front of your chest and be ready for their ball to bounce off it. All the power your opponent put into their shot will rebound right back at them, giving them a taste of their own pickly medicine.

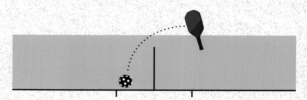

DEEP RETURN SERVE

This core shot keeps your opponents near the baseline, but if you misjudge the distance then you run the risk of hitting your ball out of bounds. Most deep return serves are hit with the forehand and aimed at the opponent's backhand. As soon as you've hit the ball you will want to run forward towards the net, but don't lose sight of the ball – you'll need to be ready to hit it as soon as it's coming back your way. Think of this move as the pickleball version of that old schoolyard classic, Red Light, Green Light.

BACKHAND ROLL

Similar to a backhand flick, this is the favourite shot of pickleball GOAT Ben Johns. Though it can be used to attack, it's also a great defensive shot to have up your sleeve, since it can be a particularly handy shot for returning low balls. This speedy dink shot uses a topspin, making it a tricky shot to return.

> **'YOU CAN USE THE ROLL TO CATCH YOUR OPPONENTS OFF-GUARD.'**
> — Pro pickler Ben Johns

BACKHAND LOB

If your opponent is near the net and taking charge of the game, pull out the backhand lob to push them back. This lob should be hit from near the kitchen, with a high arc aimed deep into their court, giving you time to position yourself well and regain control.

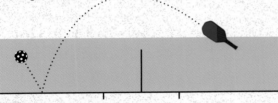

ERNE

The Erne is so controversial, it's almost a must for the serious pickler. Whizzing around the side of the kitchen and smashing the ball legally is just about the most aggressive shot you can play. 'What madness is this?' you exclaim, 'How can one volley in the kitchen?' Well, technically, you're not in the kitchen! The kitchen is 2D, and to execute an Erne, you need to either run around the side, jump over the kitchen and land outside it before you hit the ball, or hit it while you are in mid-air and then land outside the lines. Pull off this move, and you'll be leaving your opponent stunned.

SHOWBOATING

If you want to really strut your stuff on the court, incorporate some of these flashier shots into your repertoire. But don't get too cocky — the more you show off, the harder your opponent is going to try to obliterate you.

THE DINK FAKE

'What wizardry is this? You say dink and then drive me? I'm going to need therapy after all this messing with my head!' Use the same technique as your dink, but make a sudden, sharp drive, and don't be afraid to aim at your opponent's feet to make sure of the point.

CENTRELINE ACE

If you have a powerful topspin serve, this is the shot for you. Leave your opponent speechless as your ball smashes into the centreline and bounces past them before their feet have time to react. Instead of aiming your serve at your usual spot in their service court, aim for the centreline and give it the biggest thwack you can muster.

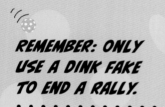

REMEMBER: ONLY USE A DINK FAKE TO END A RALLY.

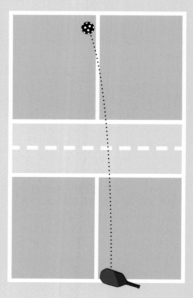

TRY A TOPSPIN VOLLEY IN RESPONSE TO YOUR OPPONENT'S THIRD SHOT DROP.

TOPSPIN VOLLEY

Also known as a roll volley, bring out this baby when your opponents have hit you a low ball but you want to keep them at the baseline. It takes dedication and skill to get this shot right, but if you can master it, you'll raise your game to a whole new level. To pull it off, you'll need to take the shot just below net height from near the kitchen line. Make contact with the ball while it is in front of you, getting your paddle under the ball and swinging upwards. The ball's spin and speed will make it harder for your opponent to return.

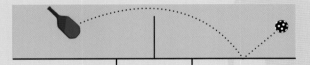

CHAINSAW

This controversial serve has been ruled illegal since 2022. Made famous by pro player Zane Navratil, it allowed the server to generate spin on the ball by using the paddle, making for a faster, more powerful game. Since the ban, players are not allowed to put spin on the ball when dropping it to the ground to bounce before hitting it. The pro-chainsaw players say that the game needs to evolve and adapt, while the anti-chainsaws say the serve changes the nature of the game. Which team are you?

BACKSPIN RETURN

This return of serve is likely to catch your opponent off guard. Use it if they've served a soft, fairly high ball, and wipe that smile off their face. Hitting the ball with a downward slice will create backspin, causing the ball to bounce away from your opponent, making it devilishly tricky to return. Since a backspin ball is slower than a topspin, it will also give you more time to get up to the kitchen line.

AROUND-THE-POST

Just as the name suggests, this is a shot made around the net post. If you have the chance to pull off this fiendishly difficult manoeuvre, you'll want to do a victory lap of the courts. At first glance

it doesn't look like this shot should be legal, but it is. Why? Because the pickleball rulebook says that a ball doesn't need to go over the net to be allowed – it can be returned at any height around the posts.

BACKHAND SPIN DINK

The ideal sneaky cross-court dink if you're in a position to attack. The spin on this ball will make it difficult for your opponent to predict where the ball will go after it bounces, and they'll have very little time to react. Unless your opponent has razor-sharp reflexes, there's a good chance they will botch their return.

UNDERSTANDING SPIN

Achieving controlled and consistent spin on your shots takes time and practise, but can really level up your game. Topspin shots result in a lower bounce, making them more difficult to return than a flat shot. A backspin will make a ball fly through the air more slowly, giving you more time to ready yourself for the return.

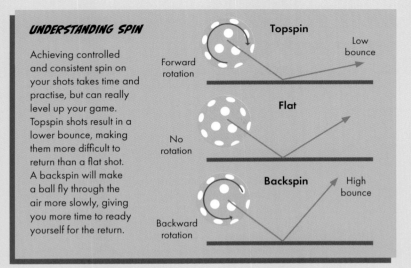

Topspin

Forward rotation

Low bounce

Flat

No rotation

Backspin

Backward rotation

High bounce

THE SCORPION

If the ball is coming towards your head or higher, instead of hitting a classic overhead volley into the left side of the court (assuming you're playing right-handed), twist your forearm to hit the ball towards the right side. This is a misdirection shot that can surprise your opponent and cause them to make an error, since they'll be expecting your shot to go the other way.

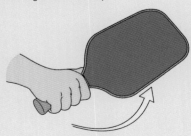

THE KYLE

While this deceptive shot has been nicknamed 'The Kyle', Kyle Yates himself claims that he learnt it from other players who have been playing with it for years. To pull off this nifty shot, come in with your paddle as though you are about to hit a low backhand, then flip your paddle around at the last minute to hit a forehand, sending the ball off in the opposite direction.

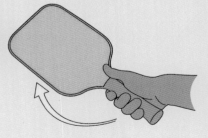

WHAT TO SAY TO YOUR PARTNER...

Good communication on the pickleball court is the key to success. What's more, use the right calls and you'll sound like a pro, even if you've only been playing since you made that New Year's resolution to lose 4.5kg (10lbs). Be careful, though: saying the wrong thing could lose you the match or, worse, your teammate.

'BOUNCE IT!' If you think that a ball is going to land out of bounds, call 'Bounce it!' or 'Let it go!' to your partner to let them know they should let the ball bounce before hitting a return. This can be clearer than saying 'Out!', which could be confused with a line call.

'OPA!' This is called when the third shot has been hit. It announces that open volleying has begun.

'ME!' or **'YOU!'** Let your partner know if you intend to take a shot or they should. It saves you from crashing into each other trying to return a shot in the middle of the court.

'OUT!' When this is called by a player before a ball has bounced, it means that player is warning their partner not to hit the ball because they think it is going to go out. If 'Out!' is called after the ball has hit the ground, it is a line call and the ball is now dead. The person who called it is indicating that they saw the ball hit the ground outside of the court lines.

'NICE TRY!' Be positive. Be generous. It really doesn't cost you anything and you and your partner will both have a better game for it.

GREAT SHOT!

...AND WHAT NOT TO SAY

'YOU SHOULD HAVE LET THAT ONE GO!' Hindsight is 20/20. Don't chew your partner's ear off if they hit a return that you think would have been called out. You wouldn't like it if they did it to you. So bite your tongue and remember this rhyme: 'While the ball's in play, shout away. When the ball is dead, keep it in your head.'

'I COULD HAVE MADE THAT SHOT!' Maybe. Maybe not. Sometimes your partner is going to mess up. It happens to the best of us. Breathe deep, and don't show your frustration.

'FOR GOODNESS SAKE, STEP UP TO THE KITCHEN LINE ALREADY!' Keep your knee-brace on and mind your manners. It's only pickleball, after all. As the T-shirt slogan says, the nicest people on Earth play pickleball.

ARE YOU TRYING TO LOSE?!

81

CROSSING THE LINE:
A GUIDE TO ETIQUETTE

It's well known that pickleballers are a friendly bunch... or are they? Just how far do you want to test their sportsmanship and hospitality? If you're new to the sport and trying to navigate your way around the court without committing a faux pas, consider this list your Pickleball Etiquette 101.

GREET YOUR FELLOW PLAYERS.

If you've never played together before, introduce yourself.

AT THE END OF A GAME, come up to the net and thank

your opponents. If your game had a referee or linespeople, thank them too.

IF IN DOUBT, DON'T CALL IT OUT.

A ball should be called in unless you're absolutely certain it was out and you can see a space between the ball and the line. Remember, you reap what you sow — if you argue every line call, your opponents aren't going to give you any slack either.

ADMIT IT WHEN YOU OR YOUR PARTNER HAS COMMITTED A FAULT.

Don't be overzealous in calling out your opponent's faults, unless you think they really aren't playing fair.

IF YOU FEEL YOU MUST QUESTION A CALL,

stay respectful and don't get into an argument.

DON'T CALL A HINDER UNLESS IT IMPACTS YOUR GAME.

DON'T GIVE OUT UNSOLICITED ADVICE.

DON'T HOG THE COURTS.

If you're playing on public courts and they're busy, remember to let others play too. Just because you got there first doesn't mean you should play for two hours straight.

IF YOU'RE AN EXPERIENCED PLAYER, don't refuse to play with beginners. Yes, you won't want to play with them all the time, but if they are never allowed to play with higher-rated players, they won't be able to improve. Beginners, don't forget this once you've got a few years of pickleball under your belts!

IF YOU'RE AN EXPERIENCED PLAYER playing a weaker opponent, don't excessively target them.

IF YOU'RE AN INEXPERIENCED PLAYER, don't pressure an advanced player into a game with you. If they aren't keen, let it go.

AS A SPECTATOR, don't shout, talk or act in a way that will distract players. Behave the way you would want others to while you are playing.

> I SAY, IT'S BEEN AN ABSOLUTE HONOUR TO PLAY YOU. REALLY TOP NOTCH!

REMEMBER: PICKLEBALL IS ULTIMATELY ABOUT HAVING A GOOD TIME. IT'S NO GOOD BEING A WINNER IF NO ONE WANTS TO PLAY WITH YOU. WIN OR LOSE, STAY FRIENDLY.

WHAT'S YOUR WARM-UP STYLE? THE 6 TYPES OF PICKLE WARM-UP

THE EXAGGERATING LUNGER

This is what Lycra was designed for. Nothing is more satisfying than a really good lunge, preferably with sound effects. Ooooh, yeah, that's the ticket. There's no way you're going to be stiff tomorrow.

THE INSTA-STRETCHER

Does it even count as a warm-up if you haven't edited it into a 10-second clip with an added soundtrack and shared it with your 20k followers? No, of course it doesn't. Now could you film my leg swings from a different angle? That one makes my calves look weird.

THE QUICK-HAM-STRETCH-AND-GO

Ugh, who has time to stretch properly when there's pickleball to play?! Let's get started and worry about our stiff quads tomorrow. If we're not quick, the courts are going to fill up and we'll end up playing with Huffing Herman, the argo-pickler that can't resist shouting at you every time you miss a return.

THE HYDRATOR

Lunge, rotate, hydrate! Even the best warm-up routine is useless if every cell in your body is crying out for water. Combat dehydration with a slurp of water after every stretch, and make sure to tell everyone that they need to watch their fluid intake.

NEVER STRETCH A COLD BODY. GET YOUR HEARTRATE UP AND WARM YOUR BODY WITH A GENTLE JOG BEFORE YOU BEGIN STRETCHING.

THE BY-THE-BOOK STRETCHER

The exact same stretches in the exact same order for the exact same number of minutes. Why mess with perfection? Woe betide anyone who interrupts the military precision of this warm-up fanatic.

THE FREESTYLER

Who needs to follow established stretches? Free up your mind and body! Go with the flow and see where your body takes you. Stretch like no one's looking (um, they are. They definitely are).

10 STRETCHES TO ADD TO YOUR WARM-UP ROUTINE

1. Hip rotations
2. Knee rotations
3. Ankle rotations
4. Leg swings
5. Torso twists
6. Lunges with rotation
7. Side lunges
8. Inchworms
9. Arm circles and swings
10. Neck rolls

DISTRACTING YOUR OPPONENT

If you want to play a little dirty to give yourself the upper hand, try out a few of these mind games on your opponent. Use them sparingly, though, and only one at a time. If you tried them all at once, your pickleball buddies are likely to think you're having some sort of breakdown.

Try the old 'Woah, is that Tyson McGuffin?!' **MISDIRECTION**.

Affect a subtle **LIMP**. Your opponent will think you're injured and let their guard down. That's when you crush them.

Channel your inner Serena Williams and let out some ear-rattling **GRUNTS** to show your opponent who's boss. Uuurh! Uuurh!

Pepper your match with little **TIPS** for how your opponent can improve their game. Belittling? No, surely not! You're just trying to be helpful...

COMPLIMENT your rival on their posture, their grip, their dinks – everything. They'll be feeling incredible... or perhaps a little unsettled... either way, they'll be thinking more about what they are doing than what you are. Time to pounce!

BE CAREFUL, IF YOU TRY TO PSYCH OUT YOUR OPPONENT, YOU MIGHT JUST END UP DISTRACTING YOURSELF.

TWO CAN PLAY AT THAT GAME. IF AN OPPONENT IS TRYING TO DISTRACT YOU, STAY CALM AND KEEP FOCUSED. LET THEM TIRE THEMSELVES OUT WHILE YOU DINK THEM INTO A CORNER.

. . . .

Whether you're on the offensive or defensive, maintain a nonplussed expression throughout the game. **NO BANTER**, just business. Your opponent will be so distracted wondering what's up, they'll be losing points left, right and centre. Meanwhile, you're 100 per cent focused on your game.

Stir yourself up into a whirlwind of sporting **BRAVADO**, scorning your rival's every move and egging them on to up their game. A word of warning, though: this only really works if you're already winning. It looks a bit silly if you're trailing 9-3.

MYTH DEBUNKER

As interest in pickleball gathers pace, lots of people have heard snippets about it and think they have the measure of the game. But do they? Let's separate fact from fiction and bust some of the most persistent myths.

MYTH 1: YOU'VE GOT TO HIT SOFT SHOTS

Pickleball prides itself on being a game of finesse, all gentle dinks nearly grazing the net as they drop into the kitchen. But that doesn't mean you can't use strength to your advantage. Half the fun is in adding an unexpected smash or drive to win a point while your opponent's jaw hangs open. If you're young and fit, why not put that power to good use?

MYTH 2: YOU'VE GOT TO GET TO THE NET AS SOON AS YOU CAN

Yes, it is an advantage to get up to the net, and yes, your opponent will be trying to keep you back at the baseline, but don't let that rush you into making silly errors. Think of the bigger picture and take your time. You need to stay in control if you want to win those points.

MYTH 3: YOU CAN'T STEP IN THE KITCHEN UNTIL THE BALL HAS BOUNCED

You must not volley in the non-volley zone (the clue is in the name, duh!) but that doesn't mean you can't hit the ball from within it at all. You can stand inside the kitchen and hit the ball, so long as it has bounced.

WHAT'S THE WEIRDEST THING YOU'VE HEARD SOMEONE CLAIM ABOUT PICKLEBALL?

• •

MYTH 4: IT'S FOR OLD PEOPLE

Pickleball may have taken off in retirement communities, but it's long since broken free. The average age of a pickleball player is 38 and falling, and around 29 per cent of pickleball players are age 18 to 34. The great thing about pickleball is that the young, old and everyone in between can play. What's more, if you're a young person competing against an experienced senior, you might just discover that they can wipe the floor with you.

MYTH 5: PICKLEBALL ISN'T A PROPER SPORT

Because pickleball is a relatively new sport, beloved of older people, and hasn't yet garnered big prize money or a lot of TV air time, many people (especially disgruntled tennis players) don't consider it a real sport. But hang on a minute – if darts is a sport, if snooker is a sport, and if breakdancing is a sport, then why the dink isn't pickleball a real sport?! Yes, many people play just for fun, but that doesn't mean it doesn't take skill and fitness. Many players are fiercely competitive, joining the hundreds of tournaments that are popping up all over the place.

MYTH 6: IT'S NOT PROPER EXERCISE

Has anyone who says this actually played pickleball? Sure, you can hit a few dinks back and forth without breaking a sweat, but most players will find themselves sprinting back and forth across the court, their hearts pounding with a heady mixture of exertion and excitement.

'IN PICKLEBALL, WITH THE COURT BEING SO SMALL, IT'S A LOT MORE SOCIAL. YOU'RE IN YOUR OPPONENT'S FACE.'

– Pro pickler Tyson McGuffin

CHAPTER FOUR

STRATEGY

In pickleball, brute force will only get you so far. To win, you need to use your wiles.
This game is a battle of wits, precision and patience. Do you have what it takes to
rattle your opponent, winning rally after rally while they dance to your tune?
Once you've boned up on these key strategies, you'll be well on your way...
just don't lend this book to your opponent.

A PICKLEBALLER'S GUIDE TO FITNESS

The right fitness regime will depend on your base level of fitness. If you've recently taken up pickleball but are more accustomed to lounging on the sofa than hitting the gym, it's wise to start slowly. Gradually build your fitness and stamina over time to avoid injury and ensure steady progress.

To maximise your pickling prowess, focus on improving key fitness factors such as stamina, strength, flexibility, and injury prevention.

CARDIOVASCULAR EXERCISE

You could have the sweetest backspin dink on the courts, but it wouldn't do you any favours if you're out of puff before there's even been a change of serve. Improve your strength and stamina by including some aerobic exercise alongside your pickle practice. Walking, hiking, running, cycling and swimming will all do the trick, and they might give you a few more years on the courts as well.

PICKLEBALL DRILLS AND PRACTICE

If you're just starting out on your pickleball journey, you'll want to get as many practice games in as possible to get a handle on the game and learn from your opponents. But once you've gained some experience, start honing your skills with drills to pin-point problem areas and gain muscle memory.

STRETCHES

To help prevent injury, commit yourself to a warm-up routine before an exercise session or pickleball game and a cool-down after.

DON'T OVERDO IT. THE PICKLEBALL COURTS MAY BE CALLING TO YOU, BUT IF YOU PLAY EVERY DAY, YOU WON'T GIVE YOUR BODY TIME TO REST.

HYDRATION

Optimise your performance by maintaining good hydration. It sounds so simple, but it's easy to wait until you're gasping for water before you reach for a glug. Do your body a favour by topping up its levels ahead of any strenuous activity.

HEALTHY DIET

Okay, if you've burnt 10 million calories in your spinning class this week, you can probably treat yourself to a desert. But for peak pickling performance, ensure your diet contains plenty of fruit and veg, wholegrains and lean proteins.

HEALTHY MIND

Physical health improves mental health. Fresh air and exercise will do wonders for your mood and concentration – just what you need if you want to focus your efforts on beating your opponents with silky-soft dinks and well-placed lobs. If you want to really maximise your performance, try incorporating yoga and meditation into your weekly routine.

SHADOW DRILLS

To get the hang of a new shot, try it out with a shadow drill first. Mimic the shot without hitting a ball. This will help you to focus on your grip, positioning, footwork and technique. Repeat the movement several times until you feel comfortable with it.

THE POLITICS OF PARTNERSHIPS

The likelihood is you know your pickling partner well. Perhaps too well. You know everything that's great about them, and similarly you're aware of their fallibilities. Here's how to maintain a healthy on-court partnership, so it doesn't affect your off-court relationship.

'IT WAS PROBABLY MY FAULT'

People make mistakes, fluff shots, net dinks, and get in your way. Practise zen-like altruism when this happens. Take a deep breath, count to three and console your partner about their misfortune. Perhaps even take the rap yourself. You'll be a better person for it, and karma will owe you one! Having done so, move calmly into position for the next point, where you will reap dreadful revenge on your adversaries for their luck.

IT'S GOOD TO TALK

Constant talk not only tells your partner what's happening, it annoys the opposition! Plenty of 'good shots', 'mine', 'out' and general positive chatter is bound to wind up your opponents.

WHEN TO GIVE ADVICE

Possibly never if it's about your partner's failings. If you're getting hammered by drives from the other side of the net because your partner's offering them up juicy volleys, make it sound like their weakness, something along the lines of 'they're struggling to hit it at their feet'. Feel free to have a post-match post-mortem over a glass of something cheeky when the heat's out of the situation.

POSITIVE MESSAGES FOR YOUR PARTNER

'I NEVER WOULD HAVE GOT THAT.'

'WHERE DID YOU LEARN TO DINK SO SPLENDIDLY?'

WHO'S GOT THE MIDDLE?

It should be the easiest part of the court to govern, but a simple shot down the middle of the court can leave you both politely leaving it to one another, and no one plays a shot. Agree beforehand on the strategy. Perhaps the player on the forehand (if you're both right or left handed) will take these unless they are out of position and there's a clear winner to be had from the other player.

'I'D HAVE CALLED THAT OUT TOO.'

'ANYONE CAN NET FROM ONE FOOT AWAY.'

PICK CAREFULLY

Do you want someone with the same mindset and skillset as you, or do you want someone to plug the gaps in your game? Perhaps you want an alpha team of drivers and smashers? Plump for the guy with the headband and the short shorts. If you want someone with a reliable dink, then perhaps the lady who's been playing badminton most of her life has the precision for you.

'HAD YOU HAVE CONNECTED, IT WOULD HAVE BEEN UNSTOPPABLE.'

'REMINISCENT OF FEDERER IN HIS POMP.'

TEARS, TANTRUMS AND THE BEST RANTS

There's always one who hasn't got past the toddler phase and would rather throw a fit – and their paddle – when they start losing, rather than suck it up. Don't be that person. If you're losing your cool, take a deep breath and a minute or two break from the game to calm down.

TOP 3 RANTS

The **'I HATE PICKLEBALL ANYWAY AND YOU'RE ALL LOSERS FOR PLAYING IT!'** This catchy number is normally brought out after the rage-filled player has smashed their paddle and stomped on it for good measure. They know you're not going to invite them to play with you again so they're going to throw that rejection right back at ya.

The **'YOU IDIOTS DON'T UNDERSTAND THE RULES!'** Every time someone calls this player up on their foot positioning or calls a fault, they have an argument ready. It seems like no one has put in as much dedication to memorizing the rule book as this zealot. If only they could put the same effort into working on their social skills.

The **'ARE YOU ACTUALLY BLIND?! THAT BALL WAS IN!'** This refrain normally comes out when the score is tantalizingly close. Funny how the ranter's own eyesight is so pickling perfect that they can see right through the back of their head.

IF YOU REALLY CAN'T HELP YOURSELF, MAKE SURE YOUR RANT IS A GOOD ONE. THE KIND THAT GOES DOWN IN HISTORY. THEN LAUGH AT YOURSELF AFTERWARDS.

BRING OUT THE DAD JOKES

If everything's getting a bit much, why not diffuse the tension with a corny joke? They do say laughter is the best medicine...

'WHY WOULDN'T THE PICKLEBALL PADDLE DATE THE TENNIS RACKET? THERE WERE TOO MANY STRINGS ATTACHED.'

'WHY IS A GOOD PICKLEBALLER A BAD PARTNER? THEY NEVER SET FOOT IN THE KITCHEN.'

'WHAT DID DESCARTES SAY WHEN HE TRIED OUT PICKLEBALL? I DINK, THEREFORE I AM.'

'HOW DO YOU KNOW IF SOMEONE'S A PICKLEBALLER? THEY TELL YOU. ALL. THE. TIME.'

'WHY DID THE PICKLEBALLER STUMBLE INTO THE NET? THEY HAD A DINKING PROBLEM.'

HOW TO KEEP COOL WHEN YOU'RE DYING INSIDE

Things not going well? Are you about to crash and burn? Sometimes, the biggest difference between players isn't their ability but their mental resilience. Make sure you have some tools up your sleeve to help you stay calm when the game isn't going your way.

CALM BEFORE THE STORM

Work your way through a calming breathing routine ahead of a game. Though you probably won't need it in a friendly game with your pickle pals, running through it in a low-stress situation will help embed it for when you're about to head onto the court for a tournament match.

PRE-MATCH BREATHING EXERCISE
- Breathe in through your nose and out through your mouth.
- Breathe in deeply, gently and slowly, counting from one to five.
- Slowly breathe out, again counting from one to five.
- Repeat this for five minutes.

> 'WHEN YOU'RE IN THE HOLE, YOU HAVE TO STAY POSITIVE BECAUSE YOUR OPPONENT'S TRYING TO BEAT YOU, AND IF YOU'RE TRYING TO BEAT YOURSELF TOO, THEN THAT'S TWO AGAINST ONE.'
>
> – Pro pickler Anna Leigh Waters

GIVE YOURSELF A PEP TALK

Don't let that negative voice in your head take over. Repeat positive messages to yourself to remind you of your strengths. Remember, it's only a game. It's only a game...

CONTROL YOUR BREATHING

If you feel yourself getting worked up and your nerves are taking over, focus on your breathing. Deep, slow breaths will help regulate your nervous system.

TAKE YOUR TIME

Feel yourself getting flustered? Take a moment to calm your breathing. If it's your serve, don't rush to get it over and done with – take your time to get your positioning right, think through your game plan, and take back control of the game.

STAY IN THE MOMENT

Don't dwell on that stumble or missed return. Instead, focus on getting in position for your next shot.

THE PUPPET ON YOUR STRINGS: KEEPING YOUR OPPONENT ON THE DEFENSIVE

Knowing how to hold your paddle and hit a few different shots will only get you so far. To be a true genius on the pickleball court you must have strategy. Like a game of chess, a great pickleballer will always have just the right shot up their sleeve to keep their opponent on the back foot.

PICKLEBALL 101

You can memorize shots from YouTube all you want, but until you master the basics, you won't stand a chance on the court.

1. Keep your eyes on the pickleball.
2. Communicate with your partner.
3. Move your feet and bend your knees – this will improve your shot placement.
4. Expect the pickleball to come back – even if you took a great shot.
5. Keep your paddle up in front of your body so you are ready for the ball.
6. Be patient – don't try to attack balls below the net.
7. Keep the pickleball low, but above the net.
8. Dodge balls that are going to be out – don't give your opponents an advantage by trying to return them.
9. Variety is your friend – mix up your shots so your opponents can't predict your moves.

'A GOOD DEEP SERVE WILL HELP YOU IN SINGLES AND DOUBLES.'

– Pro pickler Anna Leigh Waters

HITTING A HIGH BALL THAT REACHES THE BASELINE IS MORE ADVANTAGEOUS THAN SMASHING OUT A FAST SERVE THAT LANDS TOO FAR INSIDE THE BASELINE.

GET TO THE NET

Whether you're playing singles or doubles, the key strategy in pickleball is to try to get your team to the net as quickly as possible, and to keep your opponents away from the net.

GO DEEP

If you can serve deep in the court, you'll push your opponent back past the baseline. They'll need to cover more ground and use more power to keep up the rally. Likewise, if you can achieve a deep return, that will give you the maximum time to get to the kitchen line.

AIM FOR THE FEET

If your ball lands near your opponent's feet, they're going to have trouble returning it without sending it high. Therefore, aim for their feet wherever they are on court.

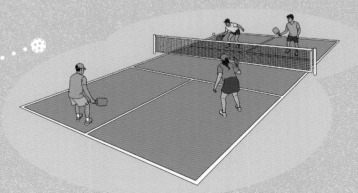

TO LOB OR NOT TO LOB...
THAT IS THE QUESTION

Each time your opponent returns the ball, you have to make a split-second decision about what shot to take. Can you volley, or should you wait for the ball to bounce? Do you go for a power shot, or will you try to take the wind out of your opponent's sails? Are you patiently keeping the rally going, waiting for your rival to slip up, or will you take a risk to end the point? Whatever you do, don't take your eye off the ball.

SINGLES STRATEGY

In a singles match, players have to cover more ground to get to the ball. Here are three tips to keep in mind if you want to avoid getting pickled.

Serve near the T. Serving near the middle of the baseline will restrict your opponent's angles when they return the shot and will reduce the amount of time it takes you to prepare for the next shot.

Switch their direction. To keep your opponent on their toes, hit shots in the opposite direction to their momentum. This will slow them down as they are forced to change course.

Go for their weakness. Hit towards your opponent's weaker side. Often — but not always — this will be their backhand.

'UNTIL YOU MAKE CONTACT WITH THE BALL, YOUR FOCUS AND YOUR ENERGY SHOULD BE ON SEEING THAT BALL TRAVEL THROUGH SPACE. THAT'S WHAT'S GOING TO MAKE THE DIFFERENCE.'

– Pro pickler Randy Reynolds

MIX IT UP

Don't rely on the same shots time after time. If you do, your opponent will be able to predict your moves. Mixing up the area of the court you're aiming for when you serve will keep your opponent on their toes. Add in some different spins and lobs, and they'll never know what's coming their way.

WHEN TO GO FOR THE DROP SHOT

If your opponent is at the kitchen line and you're not, hit a drop shot. This should give you time to get up to the kitchen line.

BEATING THE BANGERS

Keep those beastly bangers at the baseline by hitting low volleys that they can't intercept before the ball bounces. As the banger starts to move towards the kitchen, continue to aim near their feet and then aim for open sections of the court with your own aggressive shots.

103

DINK TO VICTORY

Pickleball at its best is a game of delicate dinks played with finesse and patience... and of course with the odd overhead smash or centreline ace thrown in to mix things up. If your game is more dink than drive, here are some key strategies to keep in mind.

LET YOUR OPPONENT MAKE THE MISTAKES

Don't lose sight of this key strategy – points are won when your opponent makes a mistake. Don't take risks that could result in a fault. Instead, let your rival make the error. This might take patience, but it will pay off.

PLAY TO YOUR STRENGTHS AND YOUR OPPONENT'S WEAKNESSES.

GO FOR THE MIDDLE

Hitting shots down the middle of the court means your opponents have to make a split-second decision about which of them should go for the ball. If you're lucky, neither of them will take the shot and it'll bounce off the court while they blame each other for the fault. If you're on the defensive and having to make a hasty return shot, it's safer to hit it down the middle than risk your ball going out of bounds.

DINK CROSS-COURT

Though you might find yourself in a dink battle close to the net, try to hit cross-court dinks where you can. They travel over the middle of the net where it is at its lowest point, giving you more room to clear the net. They're also more likely to be returned down the line to your partner, giving you time to get back into position.

'THE MAIN THING IN PICKLEBALL IS TO BE PATIENT.'
– Pro pickler Catherine Parenteau

> **DOWN THE MIDDLE SOLVES THE RIDDLE.**

RISK A SPEED UP?

If you're in a dinking battle, sooner or later, one of you will go for a speed up to try to win the rally. Don't rush it – wait for your opponent to make a mistake. When the ball comes at you at just the right angle, speed up. Ideally your opponent won't be able to return the ball.

THE EYES HAVE IT

Used occasionally, this trick c an really get your opponent in a pickle. Look in a different direction when hitting the ball. Your adversary will follow your gaze and move to where they think the ball is headed, wasting valuable milliseconds.

AVOIDING ON-COURT CLASHES

Played well, doubles pickleball is like a beautiful dance. It's a waltz, a jive, a meeting of souls who move as one. Played badly, it's more like two chimpanzees waving paddles in the air as they bound across the court, likely to smash into each other at any moment.

DOUBLE THE DINKING, DOUBLE THE TROUBLE

Many of the core singles strategies hold true for doubles, but you have the added advantage of another player covering ground on the court... and the disadvantage of having to read what that player is going to do. If you're part of an established team, you'll have had time to work out your strengths and weaknesses. If you're playing with someone new, make sure to have a quick debrief before your match.

YOU CALL THE SHOTS

Good communication is a must to avoid clashing paddles – or knocking heads – on the court. Make sure to call 'Mine!' or 'Yours!' so you each know who's going for a shot. Many a point has been lost when both players think the other will be trying to hit the ball.

LEFTIES AND RIGHTIES

The only thing sinister about lefties is the devastating impact they can have on the pickleball court. Making up around 90 per cent of the population, right-handers far outnumber lefties. But, if you can get your hands on a southpaw, you could be on the way to having a dream team. When two right-handers are playing, usually the player on the left side will use their strong forehand to take the shots that come down the middle. When you have a lefty on your team, each player can take charge of their own side. They have two forehands in the middle of the court, leaving little space for the opposing team to land winning balls.

ALL HAIL THE LEFTIES!

WATCH OUT FOR DIVORCE ALLEY

This is especially true for lefty-righty teams. It might take a bit of practise to avoid clashing paddles down the centreline – make a plan for who gets the middle balls. This could be the one with the stronger forehand, or you could simply call out whose ball it is based on who's in the best position.

STAGGERING

No, this isn't a move you do at the end of a long night knocking back pickleball cocktails. It's a technique to stop you crashing into your partner as you both go after the ball. While one of you takes a shot from the baseline, the other steps forward, ready to rush forward to attack the ball.

YOU LOB AND I'LL DINK

The secret to a great pickleball partnership is communicating well and knowing which areas each player is most skilled in. Does one of you have more power and the other have finesse? Use that to your advantage. Does one of you have a wicked backhand? Make sure you position yourselves to make the most of it.

YOU COULD BE THE GREATEST PICKLEBALLERS ON THE PLANET, BUT IF YOU DON'T WORK TOGETHER, YOUR OPPONENTS WILL FIND YOUR WEAKNESS AND USE IT TO WHOOP YOUR ASS.

TO TETHER OR NOT TO TETHER?

'Tethering' is the idea that you are tied to your partner with an invisible rope, so that where they go, you go. This can easily cause you to pay more attention to the tethering than what's happening with your positioning, often leaving a wide-open space for the ball. It can also strain your body as you shuffle from side to side. Instead, pay attention to maintaining a good position, so you are ready to move in any direction to hit the ball.

STACKING

Stacking is a doubles strategy where both players occupy the same half of the court. Often, it's used during the serve and return of serve, before the players move to their own sides. It can be a great tactic to make the most of one player's strength, such as a strong forehand, or make up for a weakness, such as not being as good at reaching for high balls. It might take some practise to use it to your team's best advantage, though. Be careful not to get mixed up about whose turn it is to serve and on which side.

DEALING WITH TARGETING

If your partner is less experienced than you, your opponents might take advantage and start targeting them, pummelling them with shot after shot. It's stress-inducing for your partner, and frustrating for you when you can't get a look in. Stay positive and try to keep your partner's confidence up rather than chewing their ear off. Use stacking to get some more shots in and show your opponents that they're going to have to work harder to get around you.

SHADING

No, this isn't a technique to keep your court cool on a hot summer's day. This is a strategy to help you move to the part of the court where a ball is most likely to be returned. If you've lobbed a ball over to the left, you and your partner should take a step or two to your left – it's more likely that your opponent is going to return it down the line. Sounds obvious, right? So don't stand still waiting for your opponent to aim the ball right back 'atcha.

IN IT TO WIN IT

To win a game, the better player should try to hit more balls. Put them on the left side, so they can cover the middle of the court with their forehand (assuming they are right-handed). If you're left-handed, you switch the sides over so that you're still covering the middle with your forehand.

THE DARK ARTS OF PICKLING

We both know you are a master tactician with the skills to back up your big talk. But why simply just win? Why not crush your opponent and destroy the notion that pickleball is a smiley, family friendly bat-and-ball game? Welcome to the dark side of pickleball.

TARGETING THE BODY is a good way to be aggressive and wind your opponent up. Hard as you can – it's only a pickleball anyway, so why are they so scared?

SERVE AS SOON AS THEY ARE SET – don't hang around and don't let them get settled.

THE BACKHAND GRIND – most people are weaker on their backhand, or simply can't play aggressively there. Keep playing it then. Serve it there. Lob them to that side. Play dink after dink to the backhand. If playing doubles, target the weaker side of the weakest player. Eventually, they'll do something rash and the point will be yours!

THE FAKE OUT – send your opponent skittering to the wrong side of the court with this audacious move. Pretend to swing for the ball before it's reached you, then swing for real, hitting it in the opposite direction. You'll have to be confident of your timing, though. Get this fake out wrong and it will be you who looks like a flake out.

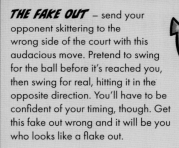

PLAY AT YOUR PACE – the serve is yours, so there's no rush. Bounce the ball a few times on the paddle, loosen the neck muscles, check the score... are your shoelaces tightly tied? Just leave 'em hanging for a little bit.

CONGRATULATE YOURSELF – if you think an opponent will play badly when wound up, then why not pop in the odd 'yup' or 'oooo' when you do a winning shot? That would annoy you, wouldn't it?

SUDDENLY GO BERSERK – lull your opponent with dinks, playing them in the style of an asthmatic octogenarian. And then let loose. Smash your hardest drives, thrusting them as hard as you can towards their feet. Be as vocal as you like, grunting with every shot!

YOU'RE THE REFEREE: WHAT WOULD YOU DO IN THESE SITUATIONS?

Are you blushing or bullish? Would you rather concede a point than ruffle feathers, or will you stand your ground no matter what? Put your judgement to the test with these scenarios.

1) In a doubles game, a receiving player returns serve but argues that a server was holding their paddle too high when they hit their shot.

DO YOU...

A) Ask the server's partner if they saw their partner's serve.
B) Tell the server to redo the point.
C) Tell the opposition that they should have made the call before returning serve.

2) During a singles match, the line judge calls a ball out and you agree. The player insists the ball was in and continues to argue their case, saying that their coach has filmed the match and can review the footage to prove it.

DO YOU...

A) Agree to look at the video to make sure your call was correct.
B) Ask the opposing player whether they think the ball was in or out.
C) Give the player a warning. You've made your call and you're going to stick with it.

3) During a celebrity fundraiser, a drunken pickleball fan stumbles onto the court.

DO YOU...

A) Let him pass out in the kitchen. He looks so peaceful. The players can work around him.
B) Stop play, have the intoxicated person escorted out of the tournament. Replay the point.
C) Dart onto the court, dodging an overhead smash and pushing the guy out of the way. Nothing should get in the way of pickleball!

4) An incorrect score is called. One of the players stops play to point this out, but only after the return of serve.

DO YOU...

A) Tell the player that although they were right about the incorrect score, after the return of serve they should have continued to play until the end of the rally. Since they stopped the rally, they have committed a fault and lose that rally.

B) Correct the score and tell the players to replay the point.

C) Correct the score and give the player who noticed an extra point and a high five for good measure.

5) A player stops a rally, claiming that the opposition has made a positioning error. You judge that the opposing player was not at fault.

DO YOU...

A) Tell the players to replay the point anyway.

B) Call a fault on the player who incorrectly stopped the rally.

C) Worry you made the wrong call and ask the opposing player if they think their position was wrong.

6) A player is standing just inside the kitchen. They jump out of the kitchen, hitting a volley while in mid-air, before landing with their feet outside the NVL.

DO YOU...

A) Applaud their quick reflexes and dynamic style. They landed outside the kitchen, so the shot was sound.

B) Call a fault. Since they hit the shot before they landed, it counts as though they volleyed from within the kitchen.

C) Ignore it and let the rally continue. It seems like a grey area...

YOU'RE THE REFEREE CONTINUED

7) It's a scorching hot day and one of the players looks like they are about to pass out from heat exhaustion.

DO YOU...

A) Pour some water over them and tell them to pull their socks up and keep playing.

B) Sadistically watch how the match pans out. How long will this pickler keep going before they admit defeat?

C) Call a referee time-out and get the player medical help. C'mon, it's only pickleball. It's not worth a trip to hospital!

8) A ball lands in the kitchen but bounces back towards the other side of the net. The receiving player jumps around the side of the net to hit the ball, but only makes contact with the ball after it has passed back into the opposition's side.

DO YOU...

A) Allow the shot. That's one nifty move.

B) Call a fault. You can't cross the plane of the net before you've hit the ball!

C) Call a time-out and frantically reread your rulebook. Was that shot legal or not? When did pickleball get so complicated?!

9) A player is about to serve, but you notice that one of their feet is touching the baseline.

DO YOU...

A) Just let it slide. Their foot is only a tiny amount over the baseline anyway. What's the harm?

B) Let them serve and then call a fault. That'll teach them to be more careful about their foot positioning later.

C) Let them know that their foot positioning needs to be adjusted before you call the score.

10) You think the server has put too much spin on the ball as they go to hit the ball, but you're not sure.

DO YOU...

A) Call a fault. You don't like that player's attitude.
B) Order a replay of the point. If you see the server put spin on the ball that time, you'll call a fault.
C) Let it slide. The chainsaw serve should be legal anyway.

11) You're refereeing a match between tennis legends Andre Agassi and John McEnroe.

DO YOU...

A) Calmly shake their hands and act professionally throughout the match. You'll ref like you've never reffed before, damn it.
B) Find yourself overcome with performance anxiety and rush off the court to breathe into a paper bag.
C) Ask them to sign your T-shirt and your cap and your shoes and your arm and you're never going to wash again. Not ever.

ANSWERS

1. C (Rule. 4.A.9)
2. C (Rule 13.G.2.d)
3. B (Rule 3.A.16 and 8.C)
4. A (Rule 4.K)
5. B (Rule 4.B.9a)
6. B (Rule 9.D)
7. C (Rule 10.H.2.a)
8. A (Rule 11.1.1)
9. C (Rule 4.B.9)
10. B (Rule 4.A.5 and 4.A.9)
11. A (Common dignity)

'THE BEST PLAYERS ARE GENERALLY THE ONES THAT ARE ADAPTING THE MOST QUICKLY.'

– Pro pickler Ben Johns

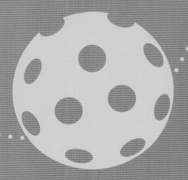

CHAPTER FIVE

COULD YOU MAKE IT AS A PRO?

Ah, living and breathing pickleball. The drills, the practise, the tournaments. What could be better? For a small handful of pickleballers, they are living the dream… and putting in the hours of blood, sweat and tears needed to stay at the top. But if you fancy yourself as the next Ben Johns or Anna Leigh Waters, what do you need to do to make it in this game?

A PRO PICKLER'S REGIME

Think being a pro pickler seems like a sweet deal? Sure, there's lots of travel, but you might not have time to enjoy the sights. For those at the top of their game, it's train, eat, sleep, repeat. Could you handle it?

A TYPICAL TRAINING DAY

- 9-10 am: gym or session with a personal trainer
- 10-11 am: healthy snack or light meal
- 11-2 pm: pickleball drills and practice games, finishing with post-game stretches
- 2.30 pm: lunch
- 3 pm onwards: time relaxing after training, as well as admin, social media, etc.
- 7 pm: dinner
- 10.30-11 pm: a good night's sleep – vital for doing it all again tomorrow.

YOU KNOW THE DRILL

For pro picklers, drills are a vital part of their training, where they can perfect shots and iron out problem areas. Some pros opt for a drill session in the morning and a gym session later in the afternoon, some do it the other way around. Ben Johns is said to spend two to four hours a day, six days a week on drills and practice games.

'TRAVELLING IS THE MOST EXHAUSTING PART.'

– Pro pickler Ben Johns

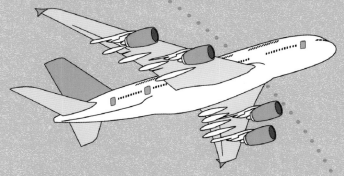

JUGGLING ACTS

Some pros dedicate most of their time to training, while others balance their practise with another job, such as pickleball coaching. For Anna Leigh Waters, who started her pickleball career at the tender age of 12, she has had to juggle training and competing with doing her schoolwork. Other pros have had to balance their pickleball careers with studying for a university degree.

TOURNAMENT TRAVEL

For all pros, tournaments and the associated travel can be a time-consuming part of their career. Most pros play at least 25 events each year. Anna Leigh Waters' routine includes travelling to tournaments every other weekend. She'll be away from home Thursday to Sunday, and then take Monday off to recover before hitting the court once more.

> 'I LIKE TO KEEP PRETTY LOW KEY. JUST AT LEAST TWO OR THREE HOURS OF PRACTICE IN A DAY AND MAKE IT TO THE GYM FIVE TO SIX DAYS A WEEK...IDEALLY!'
> — Pro pickler Meghan Dizon

PICKLEBALL HALL OF FAME

The best picklers need to keep evolving to stay at the top of this young sport. Here are some of the big names who have taken the sport by storm, raking in the tournament titles.

BEN JOHNS
Born: 1999, Maryland, USA

Arguably the greatest male pickleball player of all time, Ben's world domination shows no signs of ending. Other players can barely get a look in – in 2019, Johns enjoyed a 108-match winning streak. He's amassed more trophies than you could fit in an SUV, and was the first man to win a coveted Triple Crown. As one of seven siblings, he's had no shortage of potential doubles partners, so it's perhaps no surprise he plays with his brother, Collin Johns.

'TO BE AT THE TOP, YOU NEED TO KEEP GETTING BETTER.'

– Ben Johns

TYSON MCGUFFIN
Born: 1989, Washington, USA

Another consistently high-ranking pickler, McGuffin began his sporting career as a tennis player before switching to pickleball. Known for his agility, aggressive playing style, extensive tattoos and winning personality, this five-time Grand Slam champ and pickleball coach has been labelled 'The most electrifying man in sports'.

'WHEN I FIRST STARTED, WE DIDN'T EVEN GET PAID!'
– Kyle Yates

KYLE YATES
Born: 1995, Florida, USA

A pioneer of the game, Yates was one of the first professional pickleball players. At the age of 19, he won gold in his first tournament and has gone on to win medals across the boards. He's been touted as having revolutionized the sport of pickleball. If you're under 40 and you're into pickleball, there's a good chance you have Kyle to thank.

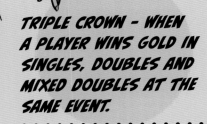

TRIPLE CROWN – WHEN A PLAYER WINS GOLD IN SINGLES, DOUBLES AND MIXED DOUBLES AT THE SAME EVENT.

PICKLEBALL HALL OF FAME

SIMONE JARDIM
Born: 1979, Santa Maria, Brazil

Nicknamed the Queen of Pickleball and celebrated for her precision and strategic thinking, Jardim is a six-time national champion and seven-time US Open champ. Now retired, she was ranked world number 1 for four years straight, from 2016 to 2020. She holds the record for most wins by a female player, with 32 titles in the Pro Pickleball Association and earning herself a Triple Crown at the US Open in 2017 and 2018.

LUCY KOVALOVA
Born: 1992, Slovakia

Hailing from Slovakia, Lucy moved to the States to play tennis for Wichita State University, Kansas. It wasn't long, though, before pickleball cast its spell on her and she swapped her racket for a paddle. Since catapulting into the world of pro pickleball in 2016, Kovalova hasn't looked back, winning the US Open five times, as well as winning gold in the singles and doubles at the USAPA National Championships. Known for her poker-face and aggressive technique on the court, off it she's a self-proclaimed fan of fashion and celebrity gossip.

'BELIEVE IN YOUR SHOTS. BELIEVE IN YOUR GAME AND WHAT YOU'VE DONE.'

– Anna Leigh Waters

ANNA LEIGH WATERS
Born: 2007, Florida, USA

If Simone is the queen, then Anna Leigh Waters is pickleball's princess. The pickling prodigy picked up a paddle aged 10 and hasn't looked back. From the outset she's teamed up with her mother and coach, Leigh Waters, to create an almost unbeatable duo. Anna Leigh turned pro after just two short years of practise, making her the youngest professional pickleball player at 12 years old. By 17 she had earned herself 10 PPA Triple Crowns, six golds at the US Open and six at the USAPA Nationals. Since 2022 she is ranked world number 1 in singles, doubles and mixed doubles. Showing her sporting talent from the outset, Florida-born Waters was set on a career as a professional soccer player before she found her pickleball calling while staying with her grandparents in Pennsylvania during Hurricane Irma. To think that if the winds of history had blown in a different direction, the world might have never known this whirlwind champion of the pickle court.

'I THINK FOR SOMEBODY TO BE GREAT AT SOMETHING, YOU HAVE TO LOOK WITHIN. I'VE ALWAYS TRIED TO NOT COMPARE MYSELF TO ANYBODY.'

– Simone Jardim

THE PICKLEBALL CHAMPIONSHIPS

Fancy strutting your stuff at a pickleball tournament? Want to see how you really measure up when you're a small fish in a big, pickly pond? With amateur brackets in many tournaments, and hundreds of tournaments taking place throughout the year, you better put your paddle where your mouth is. While most of the action happens in the United States, events are starting to take off worldwide. Let's take a look at the big ones...

US OPEN

- Takes place in Naples, Florida, USA.
- Claims to be the most prestigious tournament in pickleball.
- The largest tournament, over 3,250 players competed at the 2024 championship.
- 60 pickleball courts, including a championship court.
- $150,000 prize pot in 2024.

TOURNAMENT OF CHAMPIONS

- Takes place in Brigham City, Utah, USA.
- Started in 2012.
- First pickleball tournament to offer prize money.
- First pickleball tournament to use certified referees in all its professional matches.
- Smaller than the other top tournaments, but still prestigious.
- $250,000 prize pot in 2023.

USA PICKLEBALL NATIONAL CHAMPIONSHIPS

- Different locations across the USA.
- Started in Arizona in 2009.
- The tournament has grown from just under 400 players in 2009 to nearly 3,500 players in 2023.
- $275,000 prize pot in 2023.

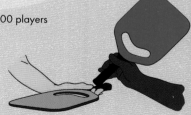

WORLD PICKLEBALL CHAMPIONSHIP SERIES (WPC SERIES)

The USA may be the birthplace of pickleball, but tournament fever is spreading worldwide. The European Pickleball Open, Oceania Pickleball Open and Asia Pickleball Open cumulate in the World Pickleball Championship.

THE PPA TOUR

- Run by the Professional Pickleball Association (PPA).
- 26 tournaments across 16 states.
- Culminates in the PPA Finals, held in San Clemente, California, where the top 8 singles and doubles players battle it out.
- Has a whopping $5.5 million prize pot.

THE APP TOUR

- Run by the Association of Pickleball Players, founded in 2019.
- Both pros and amateurs can compete.
- Features eight APP Tour Primary tournaments and four APP Tour Majors, held in Florida, New York and California.
- $100,000 to $150,000 prize money per event.
- Also includes the APP Collegiate Championships, the AARP Champions Cup (for seniors), the APP Women's Open, the APP U.S. Indoor Championships and the APP Atlantic Cup.

EUROPEAN PICKLEBALL CHAMPIONSHIP

The first European pickleball championship took place in Southampton, UK, in 2024. Dozens of smaller tournaments also take place in the UK each year.

YOUR ROUTE TO WORLD PICKLEBALL DOMINATION

If you love pickleball so much, why don't you make it into a career? After all, how hard can it really be? Here's your foolproof 13-point plan to make your pickling dreams come true.

1. Learn how to play.
2. Find your perfect paddle.
3. Practise playing singles and doubles.
4. Build up your speed, strength and stamina.
5. Work your way up the ratings.
6. Get some coaching from an expert.
7. Hone your skills at pickleball workshops.
8. Enter tournaments and push yourself to improve.
9. Pack in your day job and devote yourself to winning tournaments.
10. Get some sponsorship deals.
11. Start a YouTube channel to teach others the skills you have mastered.
12. Set up a training academy or a company selling high-end pickleball merch.
13. Retire to a super yacht with its own pickleball court.

...or you could just continue to play mediocre pickleball, have a great time and make some new friends while you're at it.

'PRACTISE HOW YOU WANT TO PLAY. PLAY HOW YOU PRACTISE.'
– Pro pickler Ben Johns

WHAT'S YOUR RATING?

Do you dream of being a champion or are you a happy amateur? Whatever your level, it can be useful to know your rating. You can find detailed descriptions of each rating's capabilities online.

1.	Beginner (absolute)
1.5	Beginner (developing)
2.0	Beginner (improving)
2.5	Advanced Beginner
3.0	Intermediate
3.5	Advanced Intermediate
4.0	Advanced
4.5	Advanced Tournament Level
5.0	Champion Level

PLAY, PLAY, PLAY

Ultimately, if you want to become a pro, you need to win tournaments. What are you waiting for? Practise, practise, then practise some more. Enter tournaments, compete against stronger players, and keep working your way up the ranks.

PICKLEBALL RECORD BREAKERS

With pickleball's stratospheric rise in popularity, it's only a matter of time before more feats of pickle prowess are attempted and more records are broken. For those keen on a (backhand) slice of eternal glory, these are the records to beat. If you don't have the power to hit a pickleball faster than a speeding bullet or the stamina to sustain a marathon rally, perhaps you could join in with the next mass exhibition match. You'll be regaling your dinking buddies with the story until they're sick of hearing it.

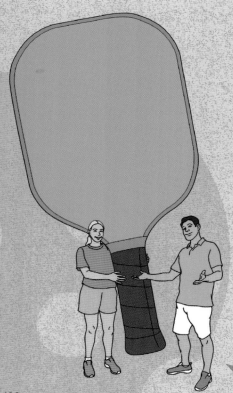

LARGEST PICKLEBALL TOURNAMENT:

Over 3,250 players
Minto US Open Pickleball Championships in Naples, Florida, USA
Date: 13–20 April 2024

LARGEST PICKLEBALL PADDLE:

4.10m (13ft, 5.4in) long and 2.05m (6ft, 8.7in) wide
Record holders: Smash Park and Paddletek in West Des Moines, Iowa, USA
Date: 28 August 2018

LONGEST PICKLEBALL RALLY:

16,046 shots
Record holders: Angelo A. Rossetti and Ettore Rossetti
Date: 10 October 2021

CAN WE GET SOME BIG BALLS OVER HERE?

THE LONGEST MARATHON PLAYING PICKLEBALL (SINGLES):

24hr 13min
Record holders: Matt Chambers and Alex Bean in Utah, USA
Date: 12-13 November 2021

FASTEST PICKLEBALL HIT:

77.24km/h (48mph)
Record holder: Joshua Biggers
Date: 14 July 2023

THE MOST SUCCESSFUL PICKLEBALL SERVES IN ONE MINUTE:

32
Record holder: Joshua Biggers
Date: 14 July 2023

THE MOST SUCCESSFUL BLINDFOLDED PICKLEBALL SERVES IN ONE MINUTE:

19
Record holder: Joshua Biggers
Date: 14 July 2023

THE MOST PARTICIPANTS IN A PICKLEBALL EXHIBITION MATCH:

264 people
Date: 5 November 2023

WHAT D'YA MEAN, IT'S NOT IN THE OLYMPICS?!

I know, it's crazy, right? How can the world's fastest growing sport not be in the Olympics? The thing is, it's not even being considered for it. It's not even eligible to be in it. The earliest pickleball could possibly be played below those five iconic rings will be 2032.

AIMING FOR THE OLYMPICS

Before pickleball can be considered for the Olympics, it will need to fulfil certain criteria. The sport must be widely practiced by men in at least 75 countries and on four continents and by women in at least 40 countries and on three continents. Pickleball might be big in North America. It might be gaining traction at an exponential rate in parts of Europe. But is it a worldwide sport? Not even close.

So, if you want to see pickleball in the Olympics, you're going to have to get people picking up paddles in all four corners of the globe. When they're lobbing in Laos and dinking in Djibouti, that's when we might be in business.

SIX SPORTS THAT WILL BEAT PICKLEBALL TO THE OLYMPICS

Baseball	Lacrosse
Softball	Squash
Flag football	Cricket

'IT MAY NOT HAPPEN IN MY LIFETIME, BUT I'M HOPING IT WILL FOR THE YOUNG ONES TO COME.'

– Pro pickler Simone Jardim

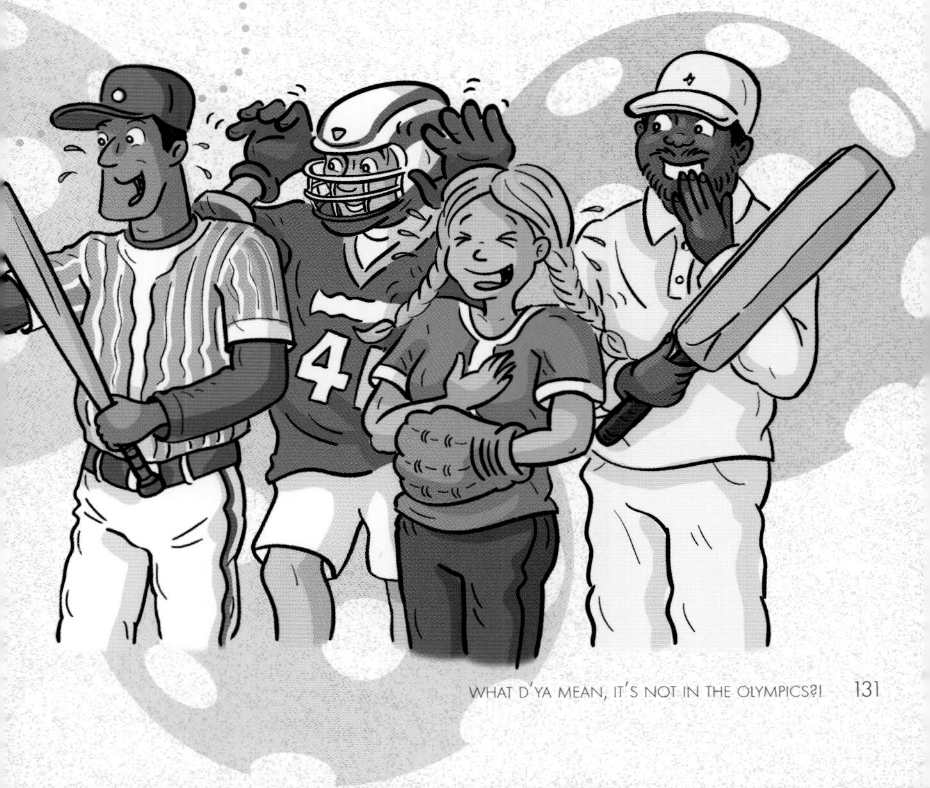
4

'THE MORE YOU AGE, THE WORSE IT GETS... I CAN'T JUST SPRING BACK LIKE I COULD YEARS AGO.'

– Pro pickler Simone Jardim

IN A PICKLE

PICKLEBALL INJURIES

Pickleball might have a reputation as a gentle sport for geriatrics, but don't be fooled. From the mild, to the severe, to the downright embarrassing, the potential for injury is limitless. Whether you're just having a friendly game with your pals or your sights are set on a tournament win, you've got to watch your step if you want to stay in the game.

IMPROVING YOUR BALANCE

If you want to improve your game and help prevent injury, one of the best things to do is to improve your balance. With better balance, you'll have better agility, connect with more balls, and reduce your chances of falling. Here are 10 ways to beef up your balance.*

1. WALKING Simple but effective. Walking backwards: also great for your balance, with the added attraction of looking like a lunatic.

2. TOE STANDS This simple exercise improves balance and increases your ankle stability – a double win.

3. GET ON A BALANCE BOARD Great for improving balance and core strength, plus it's an excuse to get a new gadget when you've promised your significant other that you definitely absolutely will not buy any more pickleball equipment.

4. STAND ON ONE LEG AND PRETEND TO BE A FLAMINGO Bonus points if you wear pink.

5. SQUATS Not the sexiest of stretches, but they are excellent at strengthening your core, leg muscles and hamstrings.

6. LUNGES This stretch will help build leg strength and balance and will increase your reach on the pickleball court. Just don't let it go to your head and start poaching your partner's balls.

7. SWIMMING Regularly ditching your paddle for the pool will help your balance and give your joints a rest while you improve your aerobic fitness. Swimming has also been found to improve hand-eye coordination in older people. Perfect if you want to improve your return.

8. BUY YOURSELF A UNICYCLE
Simultaneous juggling optional.

9. TIGHTROPE WALKING
Start off with slacklining. Progress to the Grand Canyon.

10. TAKE UP YOGA OR TAI CHI
Maybe it will help keep you zen when your partner misses their third shot drop.

*The author and publisher accept no liability for any injuries to the person or ego sustained while attempting these activities.

HOW TO FALL WELL...

If you're an avid pickleball player, it's likely that sooner or later you're going to fall. Whether you're in the prime of life or a hip-replacement hipster, don't let that misstep send you to the hospital. Here are the golden rules to minimising the damage.

If you feel yourself losing your balance and beginning to fall, resist the urge to stiffen up. Many fall injuries happen when a person breaks their fall with locked, outstretched arms.

Instead, try to **keep yourself loose** with your knees and elbows bent. This will soften the impact.

Knees and elbows bent

Rolling on impact

PREVENTION IS THE BEST MEDICINE

What's better than falling well? Don't fall at all. To minimise the risk:

- Don't play on a wet or uneven surface.
- Wear shoes with a good grip.
- Don't run backwards.
- Don't overreach and lose your balance.
- Avoid abrupt changes of direction.
- Watch out for the net and posts. Falling into these can add to your injury.

Protect your head from potential impact by tucking in your chin if you're falling backward or turning your face to the side if you're falling forward.

Try to **land on muscle** instead of bone. Your butt, thigh and back muscles can take a bruising that will be much less painful than broken bones.

Roll with it. If you can roll as you fall, this will help spread out the force of the fall rather than one area of your body absorbing the full impact. Plus, you'll look more 007 than eleven-zero.

...AND HOW TO FALL BADLY

You're connecting with ball after ball! You're on fire! You're not going to miss that shot! You do the splits for the first time in half a century. It might be another 50 years before your crotch forgives you.

In an effort to avoid a centreline collision with your partner, you try an abrupt change of direction, but it's too late. Your paddle wedges so far into your face, you think it might come out the other side.

You take such a spectacular tumble that your false teeth go flying. Your banger opponent mistakes them for the ball and destroys them with an overhead smash.

Tripping over your spotless new court shoes, you try to catch yourself but end up lurching into the neighbouring court. Time seems to slow down as you windmill your way into your fellow pickleballer, knocking him to the ground like a bowling pin. As you lie sprawled on top of him like some grotesque take on Da Vinci's *Vitruvian Man*, you wonder if you'll ever be able to live down the humiliation.

PICKLEBALL INJURIES

Some may tout pickleball as a gentle sport for geriatrics, but with four players launching themselves in all directions across a hard surface while a ball whizzes through the air, sooner or later you're going to do yourself some damage.

HEEL

Who'd have thought such a tiny body part could cause so much pain? Spend any length of time on a pickleball court and you're bound to hear the dreaded term 'plantar fasciitis'. This inflammation of the tissue under your heel is caused by overuse or overstretching. The good news is plantar fasciitis can be improved with the right footwear. Resting your feet and applying ice for 10 to 15 minutes twice a day can also help recovery.

ANKLE

With players often making quick changes of direction, sprained ankles are common. However, do not underestimate their impact. Nothing can jeopardise the tournament next week: GET YOURSELF A MOBILITY SCOOTER!

ACHILLES TENDON

Strains can be prevented by stretching and doing a proper warm up and cool down. If you tear your Achilles, you'll be out of action for a while and might need surgery to reattach it. You'll have plenty of time to compare yourself to a Greek demigod while you recuperate.

KNEE

An awkward twist or slip can tear your anterior cruciate ligament (ACL). There's nothing like sporting double knee braces to make you feel 40 years older than you really are.

HIP

Although falls can cause hip fractures, especially among older players, muscle strains in the hip area are a much more common issue.

IF YOU ACCIDENTALLY DO THE SPLITS, PLEASE TRY YOUR HARDEST NOT TO ROLL AROUND SHOUTING 'MY GROIN! MY POOR GROIN!'

HOW TO PREVENT INJURIES

- Wear well-fitting, supportive shoes.
- Always stretch properly, with a warm up before playing and a cool down after.
- Perform regular exercises to improve your core strength and balance. This will reduce your chance of falling.
- Try a lighter paddle if you're frequently experiencing wrist, elbow or shoulder strain.
- If you're feeling the strain, take it easy rather than pushing through the pain and making your injury worse.

BACK

Lower back pain and sciatica are the bane of pickleballers, often caused by repeatedly turning your body to hit the ball.

WRIST

As well as tendon strain from repetitive movement, fractures are also common, as players put their arms out in front of them to break their fall.

ELBOW

Tennis elbow by another name, pickleball elbow is a strain injury to the tendon caused by the repetitive motion of wielding your paddle. Consider a thicker paddle grip or add extra handle tape.

SHOULDER

With all that lobbing, it should be no surprise that shoulder strain is a common complaint among pickleballers. It's also possible that your sore shoulder is due to waving your hand in the air, saying 'Pick me! Pick me!' every time you try to land a pickleball game with the cool kids.

TO TREAT SPRAINS AND STRAINS, REMEMBER:

REST
ICE
COMPRESSION
ELEVATION

EXTREME PICKLEBALL INJURIES

If you're a seasoned player, you'll have seen a few shockers in your time. What's the injury that's made you wince the hardest on the pickleball court?

THE BUTT CRACK ATTACK
Ball hits you in your butt crack. And sticks there.

THE VICTORY GRAZE
When you perform an ill-thought through celebratory knee slide and strip the skin off your kneecaps. The only thing worse is the sting of humiliation.

THE PADDLE SMACK
Getting hit in the face by your partner's paddle.

THE MASOCHIST
Hitting yourself in the face with your own paddle when you take a swing but miss the ball.

THE BURST BALLOON
Heavily pregnant? Don't let that stop you. What's that? Your waters have broken... okay, maybe just finish the rally.

THE LOB GOB
The pickleball hits you in the mouth. Hey, at least there are air holes.

THE EYE BALL
Ball in your eye. So long, binocular vision!

THE CROTCHASTROPHE
Man or woman, when a pickleball hits you in your nether regions, you feel it.

VERY EXTREME INJURIES
A pickleball player in Missouri turned his head too quickly, trying to track the ball as it flew across the court. This seemingly innocuous event tore an artery in his neck, causing multiple strokes. Miraculously, he made a full recovery.

A Colorado man suffered a freak accident the first time he set foot on a pickleball court. He tripped and fell headfirst into the net, severing his spinal cord.

THE SURVIVOR'S GUIDE TO BEING OUT OF ACTION

If injury has thrown you a curveball and you've got to take some time off the court, don't despair. Put all that frustration and pent-up energy to good — and not so good — use.

WATCH ALL THE YOUTUBE

Bone up on your strategy by watching the pros. You'll be able to put your knowledge into practice when you're allowed back at the kitchen line.

MAKE SOME MISCHIEF

Come up with nicknames for yourself and all your pickleball buddies. The more ridiculous the better. Good old Frank who's known on occasion to misjudge his return volley? He's now Falafel Frank. Your pal who's always tripping up as she charges the net? Nancy 'Net Nibbler' Johnson. For yourself? Best opt for something grandiose. Your ego needs a boost right now.

GET YOUR PALS OVER

If you can't go to the pickle court, the pickle court should come to you. Invite your pickle partners round to yours for a post pickle-session drink. If you play the injury card well enough, they might even bring the snacks.

TAKE IT EASY

Even if you're itching to whack a few pickleballs, don't race back to the court before you're ready. Follow medical guidance and focus on keeping up any strengthening and stretching exercises you've been advised to do. And if you indulge in a little Netflix binging too, well, who can blame you?

SHOPPING SPREE

If you've been resisting the pull of that new pair of court shoes, perhaps now is the time for a little retail therapy. After all, proper footwear is paramount to avoiding future injuries.

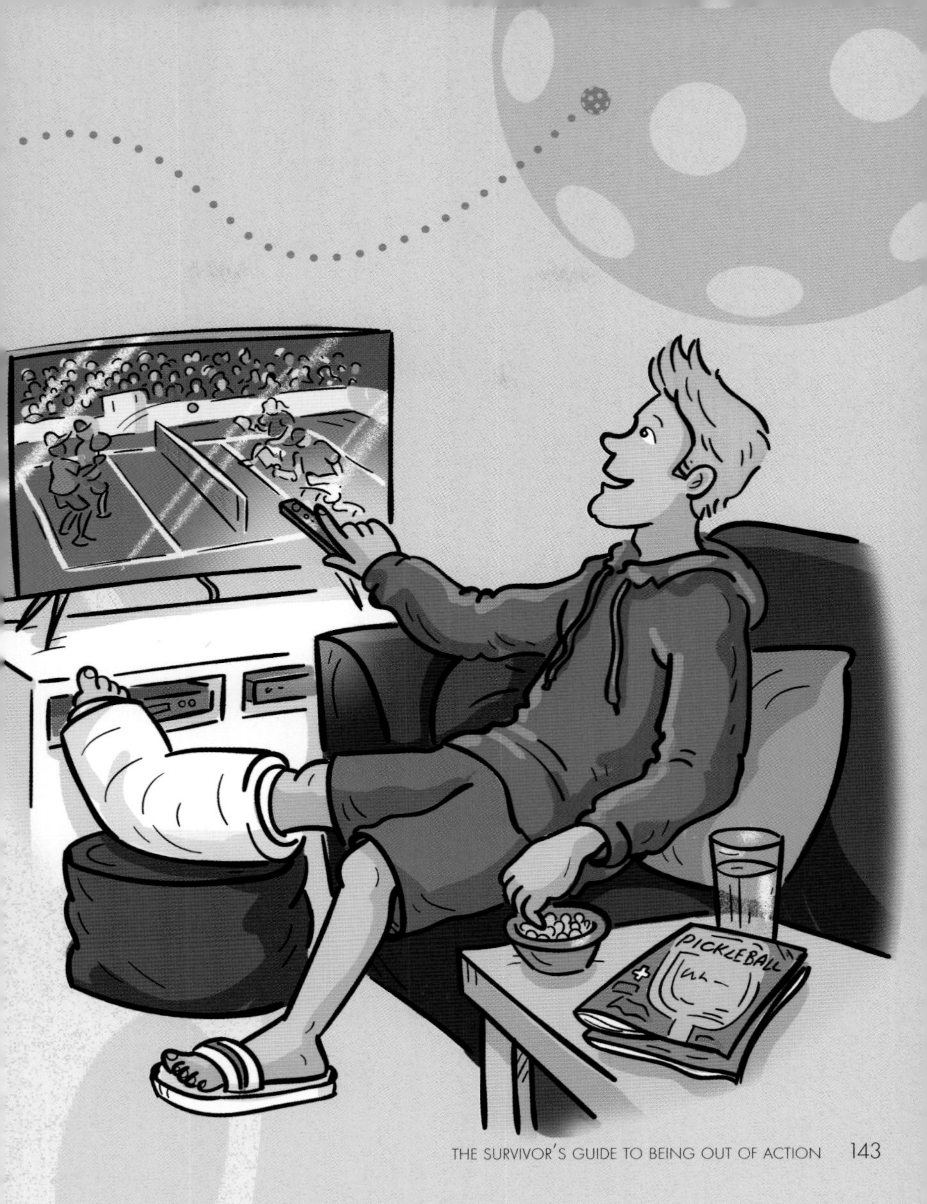
PICKLEBALL

'MY PICKLEBALL MOTTO ... IS RIP, BANG, WIN, CAKE! RIP THE BALL, BANG THE BALL, WIN THE MATCH, AND CELEBRATE WITH CAKE!'

— Pro pickler Anna Leigh Waters

CHAPTER SEVEN

APRÈS PICKLE

Let's get real. Half the fun of pickleball happens off the court. The post-match post-mortem, the heated debates with fellow pickleheads, and of course, relaxing with a refreshing pickle-themed cocktail. Whether you need to celebrate or commiserate, you should always make time for a little après pickleball...

AFTER-MATCH RECOVERY

You've pushed your energy levels, your knee joints and your deodorant to the limit in a marathon pickleball session. Whatever you do, don't skimp on your post-match recovery. Treat your mind, body, and soul right and you'll be bouncing back onto the court quicker than your dear family can mutter 'pickleball addict'.

DON'T SKIP THE COOL DOWN

We know you can't wait to head straight to the bar to dissect the match with your teammate, but a proper cool down is crucial if you want to be ready to get back on the court without having to waddle like a penguin.

REHYDRATE

If your sweat patches are bigger than the Florida Everglades, let them be a reminder to drink plenty of water before, during and after a pickleball session. Sports drinks can be a great way to quickly replenish your electrolyte levels.

MAKE SURE YOUR ELBOW IS WARMED DOWN AT THE BAR

If you feel that your cool down stretches haven't quite done the trick and your wrist is in danger of seizing up, the repetitive motion of lifting a glass to your lips can really help sort it out. In fact, it's practically doctor's orders.

HOLD EACH STRETCH FOR 20 TO 30 SECONDS AND REPEAT TWO TO THREE TIMES.

TREAT YOURSELF TO A DEEP-TISSUE MASSAGE

For niggling stiffness, a deep-tissue or sports massage can do wonders. Or, you could say you're having one, when really you're having a gentle Swedish massage while soothing ocean sounds play in the background.

BOOK YOURSELF A WEEKEND SPA BREAK

You've been working hard and playing hard, so why not relax hard too? Whether you need to recover after a string of brutal defeats or treat yourself after a great tournament performance, you can justify any luxurious pampering as self-care if you put your mind to it.

SLEEP

To give your body time to recover, make sure you get a good night's sleep. You've earned that lie-in.

OOOH, THAT'S GOOD.

FROM BUST-UP TO BEST BUDS: REPAIRING RELATIONSHIPS

Some say that marriage is the most sacred of relationships. Those people haven't played pickleball. But what if your pickleball partnership has turned as sour as, well... pickles? Here are some things to mull over if you're dinking on rocky ground.

IS YOUR SKILL LEVEL WELL MATCHED?

In any team, there will normally be one player who is more skilled or experienced. But if the difference is too stark, it could cause issues. Discuss a game plan for how to best use each player's abilities. It's okay for the better player to take more of the shots in a competitive match, but if they are hogging the court for every practice, the less experienced player might want to try out different partners.

DOES ONE OF YOU WANT TO PLAY MORE THAN THE OTHER?

It's no use constantly nagging a partner to put in more hours on the court or travel to tournaments. Have a calm discussion about what each of you wants to put into the game, and be respectful of the other's choice.

IS ONE OF YOU PLAYING TEACHER?

Sometimes it works for the more experienced partner to instruct the other, but if one of you is constantly correcting the other, it's not going to be a fun experience.

TIME TO CALL IT A DAY?

Sometimes, differences in skill level or attitude might mean your partner just isn't a good fit for you anymore. But how do you know when it's the right time to break up the dynamic duo? If one of you is less experienced and your opponents keep targeting, then it might be better for both of you to go your separate ways, at least for now. If it just isn't fun and you're worried it will damage your friendship, it could be time to (politely) call it quits.

GETTING FRUSTRATED WITH YOUR PARTNER? THEY'RE PROBABLY FEELING THE SAME ABOUT YOU!

HAVE YOU TOLD YOUR PARTNER HOW YOU FEEL?

If you're not enjoying playing with your partner, don't let the feelings fester. Think carefully about what's bothering you and what you would like to change. Discuss it calmly without blaming the other person, and listen to what they say too.

WHEN YOUR PICKLEBALL PARTNER IS YOUR SIGNIFICANT OTHER

If you've combined the two great loves of your life, playing alongside your sporty spouse, what do you do when tensions rise?

- Maybe you've been spending so much time pickling that you've neglected the romance in your relationship. Take a step back and show them there's room for more than pickleball in your affections.
- Are you rubbing each other up the wrong way on the court? Why not try playing against each other instead of as a pair.
- Are you treating your partner as well as you'd treat an acquaintance? Make sure you communicate positively instead of nagging and criticising.

DRINKS AFTER DINKS
10 PERFECT PICKLEBALL COCKTAILS

After you've served the perfect ace, serve up these dill-icious cocktails. The good times will roll further than the balls on your mate Allan's wonky DIY pickle court.

PICKLED WHISKEY SOUR

This twist on a classic cocktail really packs a punch. It's guaranteed to put the spring back in your step after a long afternoon on court. 3 parts bourbon, 1 part pickle juice, 1 part lemon juice. Garnish with a cornichon and a twist of lemon.

KAMIKAZE

If you've pulled off pickleball's kamikaze move, this is a fitting reward. You'll need something zingy to invigorate you after charging the net. 1 part vodka, 1 part triple sec, 1 part freshly squeezed lime juice. Garnish with a lime wedge or twist.

FLAMINGO FIZZ

If you've successfully pulled off a flamingo on the court, you can pull off this sparkling pink drink, inspired by the classic Bellini but with a raspberry twist. 4 parts prosecco, 1 part pureed raspberries and a dash of chambord.

PICKLED MARY

Loved by airline passengers and loathed by the sweet-of-tooth. It's a Bloody Mary with a pickly kick. 5 parts tomato juice, 1 part vodka, 1 part pickle juice, dash of Worcestershire sauce, dash of Tabasco sauce.

TURN THE KAMIKAZE INTO A REFRESHING LONG DRINK BY ADDING SODA WATER AND A DASH OF CRANBERRY JUICE.

GOLDEN PICKLE

A strong cocktail befitting a golden pickle champion. People might tell you it's a take on the Zombie cocktail. Those people are asking to be kicked out of your pickleball party. 1 part golden rum, 1 part white rum, 4 parts grapefruit juice, 1 part lime juice, 1 tsp grenadine.

PADDLE-TAP PUNCH

After end-of-game paddle taps, serve this refreshing fruit punch from a glass dispenser with a tap. Everyone will be coming back for refills. Mix equal parts of cranberry juice, pineapple juice and ginger ale with a generous helping of ice cubes. Add a slug of vodka if you want your punch to pack a little more power.

HOLEY HIGHBALL

For the clean-living, this refreshing mocktail is holier than a pickleball. Blend and strain fresh mint and cucumber and combine with soda water and elderflower cordial.

PICKLE MARTINI

A dirty backhand spin on a clean classic. 2.5 parts gin, 0.5 parts dry vermouth, 0.5 parts pickle juice.

DAIRY QUEEN

For those with a soft serve and a sweet tooth, this mellow martini is the perfect pick-me-up. 2 parts Irish cream liqueur, 1 part vodka, 1 part espresso with a whipped cream top.

PICKLEBACK

Technically not a cocktail, but no pickleball drinks list would be complete without this lip-curling taste sensation. A shot of bourbon or Irish whiskey followed by a pickle juice chaser. Dink up!

SHAKING THE PERFECT COCKTAIL

Add your ingredients to a cocktail shaker along with a handful of ice cubes. Shake vigorously for 15 to 20 seconds. Strain into a chilled glass, garnish and serve.

PICKLEBALL SNACKS

Nothing says 'pickleball is a defining part of my personality' like serving up themed food to your nearest and dearest pickle buddies. With the sport's glut of food-related lingo, the possibilities are endless.

BAGEL BITES

Bitesize wedges of bagel topped with cream cheese and smoked salmon. The perfect amuse-bouche in honour of that one time you beat your opponents 11-0. You wouldn't want them to forget it.

FALAFEL BALLS

These delicious Middle Eastern delights serve a dual purpose. Yes, they fill you up after a marathon pickleball sesh but – even better – you can pointedly offer them to your losing opponents, dropping a mention of their feeble falafels that fell short of the net.

PLATTER O' PICKLES

Pickled eggs, pickled herring, pickled onions, cornichon and, of course, the classic dill pickle. Kissing will be strictly off limits, so everyone can focus on their post-match debrief.

CUCUMBER CRUDITÉS

Refreshing cucumber batons with a spicy pickle mayo dip.

LOBSTER ROLLS

Okay, this isn't one for pickleballers on a budget. But if you can afford a top-of-the-range Lobster pickleball machine, you can afford to serve up the finest seafood at your pickleball-themed party.

FOR ADDED SOPHISTICATION, PRESENT A PLETHORA OF CHARCUTERIE LAID OUT ON A PADDLE-SHAPED BOARD.

PICKLEBALL COOKIES

Homemade vanilla cookies tinted with a mix of green and yellow food colouring and decorated with raisins to give off the perfect pickleball vibe. You can also buy pickleball and paddle cookie cutters online.

FLAPJACKS

An apt energy boost after a hard day's pickling.

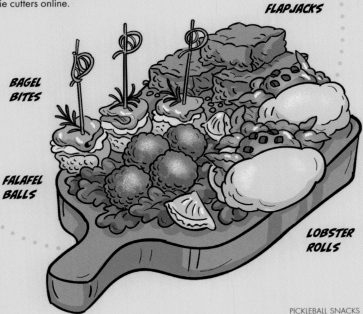

FLAPJACKS

BAGEL
BITES

FALAFEL
BALLS

LOBSTER
ROLLS

SOLUTIONS FOR THE POST-MATCH HANGOVER

If you ended up spending more time at the bar than on the court and your head feels like someone has shoved 15 pickleballs directly into your brain, then you've reached the right part of the book. Try out these hangover cures and, if they don't work, just get back on the pickleball court anyway. Your team needs you!

WATER, WATER, AND MORE WATER

Your brain is crying out for hydration. Rather than downing a pint of water, sip it gradually and let it do its work.

SLEEP IT OFF

Time heals all wounds. With a glass of water by your side, go back to bed and sleep it off. As you doze, you can dream about hitting the perfect round-the-post shot.

CARBS ARE YOUR FRIEND

Now is not the time to chow down on a platter of fried food. Instead, nibble on some toast or crackers while your stomach decides if it will forgive you for your latest misdemeanour. If you're lucky, you won't see that pickleball punch make a reappearance.

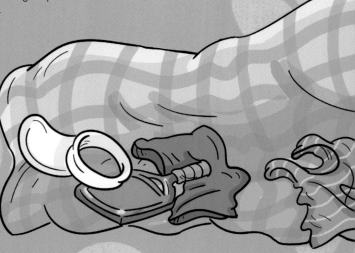

ENERGY BOOST SMOOTHIE

Once you've made it out of bed, a freshly made fruit smoothie will give you a much-needed energy boost while being gentle on the stomach. It's even better if someone else is willing to make it for you.

GET SOME CYSTEINE

If you can stomach something more substantial than toast, opt for foods rich in cysteine. Our bodies need this amino acid to produce glutathione, an antioxidant shown to help our bodies deal with the toxic effects of alcohol. Cysteine-rich foods include eggs, chicken, turkey, pork, beef, cheese, yoghurt, lentils and oatmeal.

PICKLEBALL TAKES OVER THE WORLD

There's no denying that pickleball has seen an exponential increase in players in recent years. But will its popularity continue to snowball, or will the hype fizzle out? We can see pickleball starting to take off in Europe, Asia and Australia. If this continues, then pickleball will truly be a global sport. But there are many people who argue that pickleball just isn't that great as a spectator sport. Perhaps that will change, but until it takes off with tournament and TV audiences, it'll stay primarily a participation sport.

WHAT'S IT GOT GOING FOR IT?

- It's easy to pick up
- It's sociable
- All ages can play
- It's not expensive to play
- It's more gender neutral than many other sports

WHAT'S HOLDING IT BACK?

- Not enough courts
- Not yet global
- Not seen as a spectator sport
- Not much prize money

But all that could change...

IF THE NUMBER OF PLAYERS CONTINUES TO GROW, PICKLEBALL WILL NEED MORE COURTS. A LOT MORE COURTS. AND THEY CAN'T KEEP STEALING TENNIS COURTS FOREVER.

SHOW ME THE MONEY

As pickleball generates more interest, the level that professional pickleballers play at will rise. For more people to play professionally, the prize money available is going to have to go up dramatically. At present, the total prize money given out in tennis tournaments around the world is hundreds of times that of pickleball. It will need more sponsors, TV rights and ticket sales if that prize money is going to materialize any time soon. Are there enough spectators out there?

NEW BLOOD

For the sport to continue to grow, it's not enough to just have more people try it out. We need to see players sticking around. So, if there are any newbies coming to a court near you, don't look down your nose. Welcome them with open arms – and a paddle tap.

WHAT'S THAT SPORT?

WOW, THAT LOOKS COOL!

I WANNA PLAY TOO!

ACKNOWLEDGEMENTS

THE AUTHOR WOULD LIKE TO THANK
Tom for his support and patience in discussing a sport other than cricket, and to the consultant, Bob Hutchinson, for his expert input.

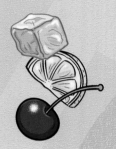